D1568997

A YEAR IN A YAWL

A True Tale of the Adventures of Four Sailors in a 30-Foot Yawl

By Russell Doubleday
From the Log of Capt. Kenneth Ransom

GAZELLE

CRUISING GUIDE PUBLICATIONS
Dunedin, Florida

CRUISING GUIDE PUBLICATIONS

Cruising Guide Publications is a special interest publisher of sailing guides to cruising in various areas around the world and other publications of nautical interest. CGP endeavours to provide comprehensive and invaluable materials to both inveterate sailors and less experienced seafarers seeking vital vacationing tips and navigating information relative to the journey to and the enjoyment of their prospective destinations.

ISBN# 0-944428-24-X

© 1995 Cruising Guide Publications

Edited by Nancy Scott

Art Direction & Cover Design by Tom Henschel

All rights reserved. No part of this publication may be reproduced, stored in a retrieval system or transmitted in any form or by any means, electronic, mechanical, photocopy, recording or otherwise without the express written permission of the publisher: Cruising Guide Publications, P.O. Box 1017, Dunedin, Florida 34697-1017.

Printed in the United States of America.

THE LAUNCHING OF THE SCHEME

In the shadow of a big apple tree four boys lay on the grass studying a map of the United States. One of the group was talking vehemently and pointing out a route of some sort with a stubby carpenter's pencil; the other three were watching with eager interest.

"That sounds all right," said one of the four as he rose to lean on his elbow, "but you can't do it with a little boat like yours. I don't believe you could do it anyway, Ken."

"Well, I couldn't do it in a steam yacht," the boy with the pencil returned, "for obvious reasons. But I can and will make that trip."

"I admire your pluck, Ken," the third boy exclaimed. "It took considerable gumption to plan and build a craft like yours alone; but I don't believe you'd bring your boat through whole."

Again they bent down to the map, and the three listened while Kenneth Ransom went over the route again.

"Yes, it looks all right on the map," Clyde Morrow broke in; "but you don't realize that the couple of inches of Illinois River from Chicago to the Mississippi, for instance, is a couple of hundred miles."

"Of course it's a big undertaking, but think of the fun. You fellows like to sail on the lake, and we have been through some pretty tough squalls, and had some mighty pleasant times, too. Sailing on the lake is good sport, and exciting, too, for a while, but

1

the cruising I propose to do makes lake sailing tame.

"Think of the places we shall see, the fishing we shall do! Think of sailing on the warm Gulf of Mexico in January, cruising around the thousands of tropical islands, then up the Atlantic coast when it is most apt to be calm, stopping whenever there is anything worth stopping for. Just think of the cities we can visit—St. Louis, Vicksburg, Memphis, New Orleans, Mobile, Jacksonville, Hampton Roads, Philadelphia, New York, and —" He stopped for sheer loss of breath.

"Why, it's the chance of a lifetime. I've set my heart on it, and I'm going. Who'll go with me?"

Kenneth had talked eagerly, so full of his subject that he could hardly get the words out fast enough. Now he stopped and waited to see if his friends would take fire from his enthusiasm.

For an instant all three boys were silent. The thought of the adventure to be had tingled in their veins.

"I'll go!" suddenly exclaimed Arthur Morrow, who had hitherto been comparatively calm, jumping to his feet to shake Ransom's hand. Almost at the same moment, Clyde, his cousin, and Frank Chauvet grabbed Kenneth and shouted, "I, too," in unison.

"Good!" was Ransom's only comment as he extricated himself from the grasp of his impetuous friends. But his face was shining, and his eyes said what his voice for a minute could not express.

. . . . .

Kenneth had been at work on his boat for some time when the foregoing conversation took place. He had planned her himself, plotting out her lines with great care and with all the enthusiasm of a boy who has the means at last to carry out a long-cherished idea.

She was to be 30 feet over all, 22 feet on the water-line, nine feet wide, and three feet draught with her center-board up. His idea was to make her yawl-rigged, and as strong and staunch as good material and careful workmanship could ensure.

For a workshop he had to be content with a woodshed at the back of his father's house, a good three-fourths of a mile from the lake shore of St. Joseph, Michigan.

Fortunately, he was able to get some extra fine white oak, well seasoned, from a nearby mill; and, though it was tough and tried the temper of his homemade tools, this very toughness and hardness would stand the young shipbuilder and his crew in good stead later.

He built a steam-box to bend the ribs and planking of his boat out of rough lumber, and made an old stove, with a section of big pipe plugged up at both ends, serve as a boiler to make the steam. Thus equipped, he began the work unaided of building a 30-foot yacht in which to cruise around on Lake Michigan and the waters tributary to it.

With great labor and care the keel was steamed, bent and laid on the blocks; then one by one the ribs were put in place. It was slow work, but it was extremely interesting to this young naval architect and shipbuilder, and as his boat grew his ideas enlarged.

To be a naval architect had been his ambition ever since he had left high school. To become a designer and builder of ships was his aim in life, and as he worked alone at his little ship, he wondered how he was going to get the experience that would be needed to design vessels for various uses and differing conditions. About lake craft he knew something, but of ocean and river vessels he was entirely ignorant. He made up his mind that he must see and study the different kinds of craft in their native waters.

One day, as he was working on the planking of his boat, the inspiration came to him. He had pulled the plank out of the long steam-box, hot, damp, and more or less pliable, and with great labor made it fast to the cut-water with a hand vise. As he bent the plank from rib to rib, he secured it until it was in place and followed the designed curve. He stood a minute facing the bow to see if the curve was true. It really was beginning to look more like a boat and less like a skeleton.

"This is going to be a pretty smart craft," he said to himself as he eyed his work lovingly. "She'll be strong and handy, roomy and seaworthy, and fit to go most anywhere."

"By Jove!" he said aloud, slapping his knee by way of emphasis, and sitting down suddenly.

"Why not?" The idea was so bold that he hardly dared to think of it. Sail to the ocean in a craft only 30 feet long? Impossible; but why? He could hardly wait to secure the plank permanently, he was so anxious to look at a map and see if there was a possible route to the salt sea that his vessel could follow.

The rest of that day was spent in studying maps, and for a good part of the night Kenneth and his father discussed the voyage.

"Yes, it is possible," Mr. Ransom said at length; "but I doubt if it has ever been done before, and certainly never by so small a boat."

"But, father," the boy pleaded, "can I go? You know what I want to do and why I want to go. It would mean a whole lot to me; it would be experience I can get in no other way."

"Yes, boy, you can go if mother can spare you," the elder reluctantly consented; "but don't set your heart on it till I talk to her. Good night."

"Well, if they won't let me go," the boy said, as he blew out the lamp, "I'll miss the chance of my life; but I think they will," and he went to bed.

It was late the next morning when the boat felt the touch of her designer's hand, for there was much talking to be done, much to be explained, and the boy found it hard to convince his mother that it was to his advantage; that it was almost necessary, in fact, for him to go on this hazardous trip.

"We can go!" he almost shouted, partly to his boat, partly to relieve his feelings, "and we'll do it, too." The boy's eyes travelled over every line and curve of his creation with a pride tempered with concern, for much depended on the staunchness and seaworthiness of his handiwork.

The fire in his makeshift furnace was soon roaring, and it was not long before the ring of the hatchet and adze filled the little shop as the boy went to work with new zest. Luncheon was a vexatious interruption, for he begrudged the time spent in eating.

The yawl took shape plank by plank, and as she grew, her builder planned ways and means, figured out places to stow provisions, water, spare tackle, rigging, and all the other hundred and one things that would be required on a long voyage. His imagination played a large part, too, and he sailed wonderful seas, through terrific storms, and along beautiful coasts—dreams, many of which, improbable as they were, would come true, for adventures innumerable and utterly unexpected were to be encountered.

"By Jove!" he said aloud one day after a particularly hard tussle with a plank that had to be both bent and twisted into position. "This is almost too much for me alone; and I can't sail around to the Atlantic by myself. Whom shall I get to go with me?"

He leaned up against the workbench to think. The yawl, almost fully planked, now stood up higher than the builder's head. The newly placed timber still steamed and gave out an odor dear to the woodworker. There was no sound except the hiss of steam in the steam-box. Suddenly the door of the shed opened and three heads appeared.

"Hello, Ken, what are you doing? Holy smoke! Look at that; isn't she a beauty!" Frank Chauvet didn't even stop to take breath between his sentences.

"Hullo, you chaps. Come in," returned Ken, making a place for them on the bench. "The very fellows I want to see," he thought to himself. "What do you think of my boat? Look out, Arthur, you'll sit on that adze if you don't be careful! You've got to look before you sit in this shop."

The third boy was meanwhile walking around the boat, inspecting her critically, feeling the wood, measuring the thickness of the timbers and eying the shape with an approving glance.

"Say, Ken, where are you going to take her? Arctic regions? She's built strong enough to go around the Horn." Clyde Morrow looked up at his friend inquiringly. "Ken, did you do all this yourself? She's great, simply great!"

"Yep—sure—you knew I was building a boat. Why didn't you come around before? Then, before they had time to answer, he went on, "Clyde, you said she was strong enough to go around the Horn; she's got to be strong enough to make a journey almost as long and quite as trying." He paused a minute and eyed his friends one after the other. Frank and Arthur were sitting side by side on the workbench. Clyde was leaning against the boat. Ransom faced them, half leaning, half sitting on a large block of iron that served as an anvil.

"What do you think about cruising to the Atlantic and back in that boat?" Kenneth pointed to the yawl. "Circumnavigating the eastern half of the United States, in other words."

"What?!" cried Arthur and the other two boys. "You're crazy!"

Clyde added.

"No, I'm not; it can be done and I'm going to try to do it." Kenneth spoke confidently and with a smile at his friends' incredulity.

"Wake up, old man," said Frank with a laugh. "That's a nice dream, but you're likely to fall out of bed."

"Listen, I've studied this thing out and it can be done. Wait a minute," Ken interrupted himself to say as Clyde opened his mouth to speak. "You know what I want to be and what I want to do, and there is no way of seeing all kinds of boats and experiencing all kinds of weather and conditions of water and climate except by seeing and experiencing them." He laughed at the lame finish of his sentence.

"The best and most thorough way of doing it, it seems to me, is to go in a small boat that you have built yourself and see everything first-hand. What a cruise it will be! I wish I could go tomorrow."

"What? Do you really mean to go?" said Frank. "Why, you're clean daft, Ken."

"Not on your life," answered Ransom sturdily. "Look here." He reached down a well-thumbed atlas from a shelf and led the way out of doors and under the apple tree.

Then, spreading it out, he began to explain what was in his mind.

THE LAUNCHING OF THE BOAT

"You shall be my mate, Arthur," said Kenneth, who from that time his friends were apt to call "Cap." "You spoke first, but to show that there is no partiality, Frank shall be navigator and Clyde chief quartermaster.

"No, I'd rather be the crew," Frank protested. "That would be more exclusive and less responsible."

"I'll vote to be cook; then I'll have you all in my power," and Clyde pointed exultantly at the other three.

"Well, none of you can be anything for a good while yet. Come and look at the boat." All four started toward the shop. "I tell you what, you can all be ship carpenters, shipwrights, riggers, fitters, caulkers, and generally hard hustlers for a couple of months before we graduate to high positions," and Ransom led on to their "*Argo.*"

After going over the plans of the boat together, and talking of all the pleasures and dangers in prospect, the four separated, Frank, Arthur and Clyde going to tell their people and ask their permission to join the expedition, an ordeal which they dreaded with all their hearts.

Kenneth lingered a while to think over the happy outcome of his afternoon's talk, and to plan anew his building, for from now on he had efficient assistants. He felt for the first time that his would be a great responsibility; for if anything happened to any of his friends, he would be to blame.

The thoughtful mood soon wore off, however, and when he locked up the shop and went into the house, he was radiant with pleasure.

"Father! Arthur, Clyde and Frank said that they would go with me." Kenneth burst into the room with his news.

"That's good," was his father's reply. "If the Morrows and Chauvets will let their sons go, that is, of course —"

"But you will speak a good word for me, won't you, father?" Kenneth smiled at him confidently.

"Ye-e-es, if you think you must go." The elder Ransom looked at his son rather sadly.

"Why, of course. I thought it was all settled. Is anything the matter? What is it?" Kenneth was excited and worried; the possibility of a final refusal from his father had never occurred to him.

"Wait a minute, son." Mr. Ransom pulled his boy down on the arm of his big leather easy chair. "The fact is, your mother and I have been talking over this projected cruise of yours, and—though you may not realize it—it is hard for us to have you, our youngest and last, go away upon so long and dangerous a trip." He stopped for a moment and looked into the boy's fast saddening face.

"We promised that you should go, and go you shall, if you insist, but you are pretty young to undertake such a journey, and your mother and I thought that you might give it up for a while. We knew that you would be disappointed,"—the father held up his hand to check the words which were just ready to pour out of the boy's mouth—"and so we thought that we would try to make it up to you in some other way.

"If you will be willing to give up your project, for a while, at least, your mother and I have decided to deed over this house and place to you and your assigns, forever," and he smiled at the legal phrase.

"Give me the house and grounds if I don't go? Father, what can I say? I thank you awfully, but I would like to think it over a bit before I answer. It is rather sudden." The boy grabbed his father's hand, and then went upstairs to his own room.

He was touched and very grateful, but grievously disappointed. He had set his heart on the trip, had persuaded his friends to go with him, and now he must give it all up. What seemed hardest of all was that he would have to tell his companions that the whole thing was off. The photographs of boats that lined the walls of the room, and the plan of his own boat laid out on the table seemed a mockery to him.

"Well, I won't take the house anyway," he said to himself. "If they want me to stay as badly as that, I won't go, of course, but..."

A minute or two later he came into the room where his father and mother were sitting reading.

"I'll stay," he said, standing before them. "I didn't know you wanted me to, so much. But I can't take the house; I don't want to be paid to stay, but you're terribly good to me."

It was hard to give up gracefully, and he dropped rather dejectedly into a chair.

"By George, mother!" Mr. Ransom said to his wife, "That boy is the right sort, and I think that we ought not to spoil his chance. I vote we let him go."

Kenneth looked eagerly at his mother. She said nothing, but he read plainly in her face that, though she feared to let him take the voyage, she would not refuse his wish.

He could not say a word; but he had to go out, unlock the door of his shop, and tell his boat confidentially what bricks his father and mother were. He just *had* to tell something.

The next morning the other three boys came with long faces and disgruntled tempers. Their parents, one and all, were against the trip, and declared that Kenneth's father and mother were crazy to let him go on such a journey.

Kenneth said nothing of his experience of the night before, but felt absolutely sure now of his parents' backing and encouragement.

"Don't you give up like that, fellows," he said cheerfully, slapping his mate-to-be on his shoulder to stir him up. "If you don't have confidence in yourself, how can you expect other people to believe in you and the success of the trip?"

"But—" began Frank.

"Bear a hand with this stick, will you?" Kenneth interrupted.

"Arthur, open that trap at the end of the steam-box, please. That's it—in she goes!" With a will, Frank and Kenneth pushed the long plank into the box.

"A few more of those, and the body of the boat will be complete. But there's a lot more to be done, and we've got to keep at it." Ransom stopped, went to a far corner, and poked among some old boards. Finally he picked out one and showed it to the boys.

"I move that we make this our motto. All those in favor will signify as much by saying 'aye'."

Four "ayes" rang out vigorously.

"Contrary-minded will signify by saying 'no.' . . . It is moved and carried that this shall be our motto, and we'll nail our colors to the woodshed."

"Hear, hear!" laughed the three at the end of Ken's speech; but when he nailed up the board bearing this motto—KEEPING EVERLASTINGLY AT IT BRINGS SUCCESS—there was a cheer that cleared the air amazingly and chased away the gloom that had bid fair to settle over the company.

"I believe that my father will be able to convince your people that our trip is feasible," said Kenneth from his place on top of a ladder. "Anyhow, let's get to work. For 'keeping everlastingly at it brings success.'" Soon all the noises the young shipbuilders made seemed to voice that motto.

It was a long time before the three got permission to go, but their evident determination and their continual "keeping at it," aided by Mr. Ransom's support, finally brought success. All this time the four worked like beavers. The planking was completed, the cabin laid out and built, the deck laid and the cockpit floored.

"Well, I'll be jiggered!" Kenneth exclaimed one day. "I never thought—how are we going to get her down to the water?"

Immediately the noise of hammer and saw, the dull clap of wood and the sharp ring of iron ceased, and all four stood openmouthed, speechless.

"Why, it's a good three-quarters of a mile to the nearest water," gasped Frank.

"And think of that hill down to the ravine between," added Clyde.

"She must weigh three tons," wailed Arthur.

"Oh, I guess Johnson, the house mover, will do it," Kenneth suggested. "Let's go and see him." But Johnson wanted a prohibitive price for moving the boat to the launching ways, so the crew decided to tackle the job themselves.

Then the trouble began. The sides of the shop had to come down to allow the yawl to be moved out, and a truck had to be built that would safely bear the great weight.

Despite all, however, the boat was finally loaded, and under the eyes of all the townspeople who could get away from their work, the first stage of their journey began.

All went well for a time. A sturdy team was hitched to the wheeled truck, and the progress over the first part of the smooth, level road was easy. Passersby were apt to quote passages about "sailing the raging meadows," and about young tars who preferred to do their sailing ashore. But Ransom and his friends were good-natured and too busy to heed anything but the overland trip of their precious craft.

When the brink of the hill leading down to the ravine was reached, the team was stopped and a consultation was held. The slope was almost 30 degrees, and a bridge at the bottom had to be passed slowly or the great weight might go through the planking.

"Make her fast to that tree," suggested Arthur, "with a block and fall, and pay out gradually till she gets to the bottom; then reverse the operation and make fast in front, hitch the team to the line and haul up."

"Great head, Art! We'll do it." And Ken started back to the shop for the block and fall.

The road curved just before descending to the ravine, and a big tree grew in the bend. A line made fast to it would lead straight down. It was most advantageously placed. A sling was put around the tree, and another was run about the boat herself just below the rail. To each of these a block was attached. The captain went over each rope carefully to see that all was right, tight and strong. Frank drove the horses, which were to back with all their might; Clyde watched the boat herself, while Kenneth and Arthur tended the line and stood prepared to pay out slowly.

"Let her go, slowly now, e-e-easy!" yelled Ransom to Frank with the team.

Kenneth and Arthur took in the slack and braced against the strain. The horses began to move slowly and the truck slid gradu-

11

ally over the crest of the hill. The line tightened and the blocks clucked sleepily under the strain.

"Go easy!" yelled Ransom.

The truck was going faster; he and Arthur could hardly hold it back.

"Easy there; pull up, Frank." The horses were straining back with all their might, but the weight of the boat was pushing them on faster than they wanted to go.

"Stop, Frank! She's running away!"

But there was no stopping her from before—the horses were fairly off their feet. The running line was beginning to burn Kenneth's and Arthur's hands. She was running away, sure enough, and to certain destruction if she were not stopped at once.

Frank's face was pale and anxious as he shouted and strained back on the reins, trying to stop his team. Clyde, utterly helpless, ran from side to side, looking in vain for a stick or log with which to check the wheels. Kenneth and Arthur clung desperately to the line, which, in spite of all, they could not control.

The speed of the boat was growing faster and faster every second. The work of months and the means of a glorious trip was going to destruction.

"Here, Arthur, quick! I'll try to hold while you take a double turn around that other tree. Quick, quick!" cried Kenneth, his anxiety almost taking away his voice for the moment.

Arthur turned to obey. "Quick—for the love of Moses, quick!"

Just in time, Arthur got the turns around the tree, for Kenneth could not stand the strain on his hands any longer and he dropped the rope. His weight off the restraining line, the truck almost pushed the horses over on their heads. But the slack was taken up in a minute, and though the line creaked ominously under the strain and stood as taut as a harp string, it held; the truck slackened speed.

"Kick me 'round the block, will you, Arthur, for a chump," Ransom said as he came up to his friend, bandaging his blistered hands with his handkerchief as he spoke. "To let a weight like that go without taking a turn was about the most foolish thing I ever did. Let her go, easy now."

The other three boys said nothing for a while, but when the

bottom of the hill was reached, all were rather limp.

Dragging the boat out of the valley was about as difficult as letting her down into it, and it consumed the balance of the daylight. The close of the second day saw the boat resting on the launching ways, and the boys were triumphant.

"If the rest of our journey is as slow as this," Arthur remarked as he put on his coat to go home, "we'll be ancient mariners before we cover the 6,000 miles."

The following day the boat was launched, and as she nodded her acknowledgments to the pretty girl who had just named her *Gazelle*, it was evident to all that the title fit her like the coat of white paint that glistened on her sides.

The hearts of Captain Kenneth and his friends glowed within them when they saw the boat at which they had labored so steadily, floating in her natural element as gracefully and daintily as if she had been born to it.

When their friends had gone, the four sat in the cozy cabin and congratulated each other with looks and handclasps rather than words. They felt that they were fairly started, now that their craft was afloat. But it was two good long months before she was ready to take her trial trip; and two weeks beyond that before all was ready to start in earnest. Rigging and final finishing took much time, and the placing of the necessary stores seemed an endless job.

"Well, boys," Ransom said, as the other three came aboard on the morning of October 27, 1898, "this is the day that we say goodbye to old St. Joe."

"Grab my bag, will you, Ken?" came by way of answer from Arthur. "Look out! If you dump the buttons from my sewing kit, I'll have your heart's blood."

"Don't you worry. I'll be careful enough," was Ransom's answer. "I'll have occasion to borrow it before long."

And so they laughed and chatted, and put on a brave front in order to conceal the slight uneasiness that lingered persistently in the background of all their thoughts.

It was three o'clock before complete arrangements were made, and all hands were glad that there was so much to do. Home was inexpressibly dear to those four boys, and though they looked forward to their trip with real enthusiasm, when the parting came they found it a good deal of a wrench.

The wind was coming out of the north in a businesslike way, and the sea it banked up was not of the sort to tempt the fair-weather sailor.

"All ready, boys?" sang out Captain Ransom from his place at the tiller.

"All ready!" was the answer.

"Arthur, stand by to tend the jib sheet; Frank, stand at the halyards. Clyde, go forward, yank up the mudhook and cat it. I'll tend the mizzen."

The boys jumped to do his bidding. The windlass creaked and the yawl began to eat up the anchor cable.

"She's broke!" came the cry from forward as the anchor gave up its last hold on Michigan soil for many a long day.

"Haul up your jib, Clyde. Now, Arthur, in with your sheet." Ransom at the same time hauled in the mizzen a little and shifted the helm.

The boat gathered headway slowly, then gained in speed till she was bounding over the rollers bravely.

"We are underway at last," Ransom half sighed; but the sigh changed to a thrill of pure delight as he felt his boat slipping along under him; felt her answer to his touch on the tiller, as an intelligent horse responds to the hand on his bridle-rein.

The graceful craft heeled over to the freshening breeze until she showed a little of the dark green of her underbody. The way she moved along surprised and delighted the people on shore almost as much as it did her captain and crew.

Out from the shelter of the river's headland she flew to the lake itself, which still heaved a reminder of the terrific storm of a few days ago.

A line of handkerchiefs waved from the bluff, and here and there a vivid bit of color showed a private signal that told of some special watcher. It was these signals that the boys looked for with particular eagerness and answered with frantic zeal. They told of loving and anxious hearts—anxious, but proud of boys who had the courage to undertake such a journey.

The *Gazelle* sped on until she came abreast of the life-saving station on the end of the long pier. The station's cannon boomed out its hail of Godspeed and good luck, and the boys lowered the ensign from the peak three times in answer. It was the last audible message.

Minute by minute, the shore grew dimmer and dimmer; the handkerchief signals faded. Even the brave bits of color steadfastly waving were lost to view.

The *Gazelle* and her crew were at last outward bound.

OUTWARD BOUND

It was a quiet group of boys who stood in the cockpit of the *Gazelle* and watched the shores of their native town fade from view. They had persevered in their scheme in spite of discouragement from their elders and ridicule from their companions. They had undertaken a seemingly impossible thing. What would the outcome be?

It was well that the young adventurers could not foresee what the future had in store for them, for stouter hearts even than theirs might have hesitated at the prospect.

As it was, none of them had forgotten that "Keeping everlastingly at it brings success," and all four meant to follow that motto to the end.

"Clyde!" Ransom suddenly interrupted the reverie into which they had fallen. "I think I once heard you say that you would like to be cook. Now's your chance. Go ahead and be it."

"My, what a memory you have," the other answered with a wry face. "But wait until you try some of my cooking, then the smile will travel my way. I'm sorry for you." And Clyde disappeared down the companionway.

The storm which had just passed left the surface of the lake very uneasy, and the little yacht was tossed from the crest of one huge wave to another like a chip, but she bore the rough usage splendidly and hardly shipped water at all. The spray which her sharp spoon bow dashed up as she flew into the whitecaps was all the wetting her deck showed.

"Say," came a muffled voice from below, "I'll mutiny if someone doesn't come down and hold the things on the stove. The coffeepot is trying to jump into the saucepan's lap! ... Hello! On deck, there! Come down and sit on the..."

The owner of the voice showed a very red and wrathful face at the foot of the ladder. Frank went below at once, and soon the sound of voices mingled with that of clattering tins and chinking pottery. Then the odor of steaming coffee and frying bacon came through the half-closed companionway.

Kenneth and his mate began to lose interest in the set of the sails, the curve of the rail and the angry look of the water. Frequent glances, thrown at the opening from which such satisfying aromas penetrated, betrayed the direction in which their thoughts had strayed.

"All hands below to supper," was the welcome cry. "Except the skipper, who will stay on deck and steer, I suppose." So the cook got even.

The table, hinged to either side of the center-board trunk, bore a goodly store of "shore grub." The ship's stove was steaming away in the galley, way forward, almost under the deck.

On either side of the cabin the bunks were ranged, good, wide bunks with generous cushions. They served as beds by night and couches by day, the bedding being rolled up under the deck and concealed by curtains. Under each bunk was a wide chest or locker, and besides, a row of drawers was built forward so that each member of the crew had ample room wherein to stow his belongings. A man-of-warsman would be at a loss to know what to do with so much space.

The cabin was 14 feet long, nine feet wide at the widest part, and six feet high. Any member of the crew could stand upright without fear of losing his upper story.

The skipper saw all this in his mind's eye as he fondled the tiller (a boat's most sensitive, sympathetic spot) and watched the sails puffing to the breath of the breeze. He grew hungrier every minute, but every minute the wind grew stronger and the waves higher, so that his interest in the behavior of his boat returned and increased, until he forgot about the complainings of his stomach altogether.

The *Gazelle* seemed to know that her maker's eye was upon her, for she showed off in brave style. She rose on the waves as lightly as a cork, and swept along at a surprising rate of speed.

Frank and Arthur soon came climbing up on deck, and then Ransom had his turn below. In spite of Clyde's protestations, he was no mean cook, and if "the proof of the pudding lies in the eating," the crew was certainly satisfied with their first meal aboard.

"How are we going to work this thing?" said Arthur as Ransom's head appeared above the hatch coaming. "We certainly won't get in to Chicago before morning."

"We'll divide up the night into regular watches—four on, four off. See?" explained Kenneth.

"But who's who?" queried Clyde from the foot of the companionway ladder.

"Arthur and I will be the starboard watch; you and Frank will be the port. That satisfactory?"

"Sure," the other three responded.

"Well, suppose the port watch goes on duty for the second dog watch—from 6:00 to 8:00—while the starboard watch does the dishes?"

"I never heard of a starboard watch washing dishes," said Frank. "But I think they could not be better employed."

Kenneth and Arthur went below and began to wrestle the pots and dishes while Frank and Clyde sailed the boat.

The yacht rolled a good deal, and the amateur dishwashers found it difficult to keep the water in the dishpan. But if the yawl pitched, it was not unduly, and she always recovered herself easily. Her poise was well-nigh perfect.

Though the off-and-on plan was carried out, there was little sleep for either watch—the experience was too new—and when Chicago was reached late the next morning, all hands were glad to lay up for a while and rest. They considered that the trip had now fairly begun, inasmuch as people had predicted that the *Gazelle* would never cross even the lake in safety.

The boys took advantage of city prices and bought all sorts of things and stowed them aboard the yacht. There was enough stuff aboard to stock a small store for a year, yet the yawl did not seem to be overburdened.

"Hear yer goin' through to the canal." It was the evening of the second day when a burly, bearded chap shouted this in a foghorn voice to Arthur. "Want a tow through, Cap?"

"Here, Ken, is a fellow who wants to tow us to the canal," Arthur shouted down the open hatch to Ransom.

They did want a tow, and the agreement was soon made, so the tugboat man departed content.

The following afternoon a little tubby, snub-nosed, paintless tug steamed up, and the boys recognized their tugboat man in the pilot house.

"Hello, Cap!" was his greeting. "Ready?"

"Hello, Captain!" Ransom responded. "All ready. Give us a line."

The hawser was hauled aboard and made fast to the capstan bitts forward, and soon the yacht was on her way once more.

All of the boys had seen the Chicago River before, but never had any of them come so close to the shipping. There were whalebacks for freight and whalebacks for passengers, steamboats, Great Lake grain and passenger steamers, little tugs towing barges ten times their size, and sailing craft of all kinds. It was bewildering, and how the little tug ever found a way through the labyrinth was a marvel. All went well, however, though the boys held their breaths whenever there was a particularly close shave, and so were almost continually in a state of suspended animation.

It seemed as if miles of craft of various kinds had been passed, when they came up to an enormous grain steamer which was fast aground. She was surrounded by a mob of puffing tugs, which had been working since the day before to get her off. The steamer and her escorts took up most of the stream, but a narrow lane remained open at one side just wide enough to allow the tug and the *Gazelle* to pass through.

There was barely room between the towering sides of the great freighter and the heavily timbered side of the river-bulkhead, but there seemed to be no danger that the great vessel would get off and fill up the narrow passageway. The boys, therefore, told their tug to go on.

The tug entered the open lane and puffed steadily ahead, the yacht following a hundred feet behind. The towboat passed on, and the *Gazelle* came abreast of the freighter's stern. It overshadowed the small craft just as a tall office building would dwarf a newsstand beside it. The four boys gazed at her great iron sides in admiration and wonder; they could almost touch it.

"I wonder will they ever get her off!" exclaimed Arthur. "She looks as if she was built on to the bottom."

"Say, Ken, look!" It was Frank who grabbed Ransom's arm and pointed to the great ship's counter. "Isn't she moving now?"

She certainly was. The freighter's stern was swinging around, slowly at first, but gaining in speed every moment. The tug was going ahead, and the iron sides were closing down on the little yacht irresistibly. It was a horrible trap which the tug, by reason of the long towline, had escaped. The boys realized their danger and shouted to the captain of the tug. He immediately rang for full speed ahead. It was a grim race to escape destruction.

Faster the tug churned on, but nearer and nearer came the terrible iron wall until it bumped against the yawl's white sides. Both yacht and freighter were edged in to the spiles of the bulkhead until there was but three feet of open water between. Men on the freighter, ashore and on nearby vessels saw the danger. They shouted words of encouragement and warning, but even as they did, they knew that it was of no avail.

Nearer and nearer the fearful iron wall approached, inexorably. The boys saw that the boat was doomed to certain destruction, and perhaps death lay in wait for them, but they could do nothing.

They were being drawn into the very jaws of the trap, and the crew looked at the smooth sides of the freighter for a foothold or a hanging rope that they might cling to, and then to the slimy bulkhead. Each had picked out a place for himself to spring for when the time should come.

Suddenly the movement of the great ship's stern stopped. She quivered a moment and was still. She had grounded just in time, and the *Gazelle* slipped through with not three feet to spare.

The shout that went up from the onlookers was like the sudden escape of long pent-up steam. It was a glad cry of relief, and the boys echoed it in spirit, but could do nothing but wave their caps in answer.

It had been a narrow escape, and the crew of the *Gazelle* were thankful enough to come out of it alive. To the shouts of the onlookers, however, they waved their caps airily, as if it was an everyday matter to escape from the jaws of death.

After this all went well. The tug and its light tow made such good time that the entrance lock to the Illinois and Michigan Canal was reached by nine o'clock. All hands turned in except Ransom, who was to take the first four-hour watch. But from time to time during the night, various members of the crew waked with a feeling that there was a house crushing them. Whether this was caused by the experience with the ship or the pancakes which Clyde concocted for supper, this chronicler does not pretend to state.

Early the following morning, the boys paid their canal fees and passed through the lock.

"How long is this canal, Ken?" Frank asked, after they had tied up in the basin.

"Ninety-six or -seven miles, I think," he answered.

"Walking good?" was Clyde's question. "I don't see a crowd of tug men crying like hackmen at a depot, 'Tug, sir.' 'Tow, sir.' 'Take you through quick, sir.'"

"You're right," said Kenneth with a smile. "It's pretty late for shipping, I hear; but perhaps that steam freighter that we heard was coming through will give us a lift. Let's wait a while and see."

They did, and the freighter good-naturedly gave them a tow all the afternoon. But good things, like everything else, have an ending, and the following morning found them towless.

A good half of this 96-mile canal the boys towed their boat by hand—they were their own mules, as Arthur expressed it. Two towed, and two stayed aboard, steered and tended ship. The starboard and port watches took turns.

The hunting along the way was good, and many a plump duck tried the carving abilities of the cook and tickled the palates of the sailors.

Seven days of towing by hand and friendly helps from passing steamers brought them to La Salle, the end of the canal and the

Illinois River. Letters from home reached them here, and gladdened their hearts mightily. It was one of the consolations of this trip that every few days they received word from home and were able to send messages to the anxious ones who were left behind.

Though the boys were somewhat footsore from their unaccustomed walking and their amphibious journeying, they were gaining weight steadily, and would have made splendid "after" pictures for a tonic advertisement.

The night on which they reached La Salle was cold, and after getting their letters, the four friends made all shipshape on deck and then went below, closing the hatch behind them. After a rousing supper to which, needless to say, they did full justice, the table was cleared, dishes put away, and in a twinkling the place was turned into a reading saloon or a lounging room.

The swinging lamp shed a soft glow on the warm coloring of the cherry woodwork and cushioned bunks. The light on the table was ample, and the boys set out to answer the pile of letters they had received. It was a great temptation to tell hair-raising tales of every little happening that they had met with, but from the first it was agreed that only the pleasant things should be detailed at any length.

For a time, the scratching of pens on paper was the only sound, other than the comfortable, subdued creak of the throat of the main boom on the mast, which made itself heard as a passing gust struck the yawl. Presently, however, one of the pens stopped scratching and its owner added a new element to the soft sounds—that of heavy breathing and an unmistakable snore.

Soon all but Ransom were stretched out on their bunks, fully clothed but sound asleep. He still struggled to write, keeping awake by force of fist in eye. He, too, was almost dozing. The gust had passed and the boom was quiet. The low hum of the lamp the only sound to be heard.

Thump, thump! The thud of something heavy jarred the four out of their doze with a start. Then a scraping sound followed and a couple of thumps at their feet. It was startling, and Ransom scrambled to his feet and, followed by his three companions, half asleep as they were, who looked about with dismayed faces, rushed on deck, expecting to find themselves on shore and in imminent danger. Instead, they found a comfortable old log with some branches clinging to it that had floated downstream and had merely knocked off some of the *Gazelle*'s white paint in passing.

"That's one on us," laughed Kenneth in a relieved manner. "Let's turn in."

When the boys got up the next morning, they found a layer of snow on deck, and a thin skin of ice on the still water. It was high time to be on their way, so they shipped their mast again, bent on the sails and set up the rigging in a hurry, and the following day were well on their way down the river towards the Mississippi.

The Illinois River is broad and shallow, and in order to keep enough water in the stream to float the grain boats down to the great river, enormous dams are built at intervals. A lock at each dam allows the vessels to drop to the lower level. Leading to each lock is a canal a hundred yards or so long.

The *Gazelle* made good way down the river, but each dam was approached with much care. A tack missed, the boat would in all probability go to her destruction.

They had but three more dams to pass and were sailing along with a beautiful breeze across stream to their starboard hand. Several hundred yards above the lock, Arthur blew a lusty blast on the horn to notify the gatekeeper of their approach. Again he blew, and at last they saw the man come out of his house and begin to work the levers that opened the enormous gates. The *Gazelle* swept on, straight as an arrow, for the gate, every stitch drawing, her forefoot fairly spurning the water, and the small boat *His Nibs* bobbing gaily behind.

The yacht was sailing faster than they realized, and suddenly the boys saw that they would reach the gate before it was opened wide enough to admit them. There was but one thing to do. With a warning shout of "hard-a-lee," Kenneth bore down on the tiller, the other boys hauled in the sheets, and in a minute the boat was heading out and up the stream. It was quick work, but for a time all seemed well. Then the wind slackened and a swift current caught them.

The boat began to drift downstream toward the dam. To the alarmed boys the current seemed as swift as a mill race. It was carrying them at a terrific rate straight for the dam and to what seemed certain death. Now they could see the ugly heads of the logs sticking out of the water at the brink of the falls, and jagged stones which turned the stream to foam in a hundred places.

Still the wind lagged and the current increased in speed. The boys looked from one to the other. Each knew that nothing could be done, but instinctively they hoped that something would intervene to save them.

But what could save them now? With pallid faces and pounding hearts, they agreed to stick with each other and the ship.

Still the stream ran on and the breeze lagged. The line of white that defined the edge of the falls could now be distinctly seen, and the roar of the water drowned all other sounds. They began to give up hope. It seemed as if nothing could help them—surely nothing could.

Ransom was watching the bit of bunting—the fly—at the mainmast head. He saw it straighten out and begin to snap.

"Boys!" he exclaimed. "There's a chance yet. Look!"

Even as he spoke, a puff of wind struck them, the sails rounded out and the backward speed of the yacht slackened. Inch by inch, she began to gain on the current. Her crew felt as if they were pushing her along; their nerves and muscles tense.

Soon they saw that they were making real headway. If the wind held they would be safe yet. It was a gallant fight that the spruce *Gazelle* made—a fight for her life and the lives of her crew, and still the wind held strong and true. She gained.

At last it was safe to come about. "Hard-a-lee," sang out the steersman cheerfully, as he headed the boat up into the wind. The *Gazelle* paused a moment in apparent indecision, her headsails flapping. Then around she came and headed straight for the now widely open gates.

AN ADVENTURE IN ST. LOUIS

Though the adventure with the dam shook the young sailors' nerves somewhat, still it served to give them increased confidence in their boat. Distinctly, a craft that behaved so well under such trying circumstances was worth sticking to, they argued, and not unreasonably.

When the boys saw how little shipping there was moving, they realized that winter was coming apace, and that if they were to enjoy the balmy south without a spell of Arctic journeying, no time must be lost. A skin of ice on the water was now a common occurrence, and it took a considerable amount of courage to crawl out from under the warm blankets and go on deck to wash o'mornings.

Therefore, the stops along the Illinois River were cut as short as possible, and only the difficulties of navigating a strange stream prevented them from sailing at night. As it was, not a few risks that would otherwise have been carefully avoided were taken in order to gain time.

At Beardstown, Illinois, they came to two fine bridges across the stream, but built too low to allow of even the *Gazelle*'s short spar passing underneath.

The yacht was sweeping along at a merry pace, wind astern and current aiding. Frank, who was doing lookout duty forward, caught sight of the upstream bridge first and blew a long, unmelodious note on the ship's foghorn.

"What do you think of that for nerve!?" shouted Frank to his companions in the cockpit aft. "Here we are, four chaps in a 30-foot toy boat, blowing a horn to have a thousand-ton bridge make an opening for us."

"Yes, we're little, I know, but oh, my!" Arthur answered. "Just give them another blow. They are fearful slow. Guess they don't know we're in a hurry."

The yacht sped on at a splendid gait, and the draw opened none too soon, for the *Gazelle* slid through before the great span had stopped swinging around. She made a gallant sight, her mainsail and jigger spread out wide, wing and wing, and rounded out like the cheeks of Boreas. Her round spoon bow slipped over, rather than cut through the water, and the easy lines of her stern left but little wake behind. *His Nibs*, towing behind, made enough fuss, however, to supply several boats many times its size. It fairly strutted along in its importance.

The pedestrians on the footpath forgot in their interest to be impatient at the delay caused by the opening of the bridge, and watched the yacht flying along, more like a live creature than a thing of mere wood and canvas.

A few hundred yards below, another bridge spanned the stream, and Frank, still forward, blew another long, "open sesame" blast. In answer the draw began to move, so slowly, however, that the crew were troubled. It seemed as if it would never open in time to let them through. But the boys figured that the draw moved faster than they realized and that the space was wider than it seemed. They therefore held on their course.

The *Gazelle*, appearing to understand that she was being watched, fairly outdid herself. Her crew became exhilarated and watched the water with flushed cheeks and shining eyes as it rushed past.

"Great Scott, look at that!" suddenly Frank shouted. "Come about, for heaven's sake!"

The other three looked where he pointed and saw that the draw had stopped moving. It would be impossible to go through the narrow opening. The men on the bridge, seeing the danger— it was growing each second so terribly imminent—worked desperately to set the machinery which turned the bridge going.

The boat was within 75 feet of the low trusses that would undoubtedly shatter its spars to kindling wood and tear the sails to rags, and still the *Gazelle* flew along, joyously careless of all save the buoyancy of the moment. She was sailing down the right side of the river in order to follow the motion of the draw, which was from left to right. The pier which supported the middle span was in midstream, a massive stone structure with a prow like the ram of a battleship, planned, in fact, to break up and separate the ice.

"Come about, Ken, quick, or you'll carry away your stick." Frank waved his arms and pointed frantically to the bridge.

Ransom paused a minute and measured the distance between his craft and the bridge, glanced at the stone pier and hesitated. He was pale, but outwardly calm. At last he put the tiller over to port and the gallant little craft swung around on her heel like a dancer. Her pace slackened, but the current and wind still carried her onward nearer and nearer the bridge, her momentum spinning her around until she was headed straight for the beak of the stone pier, jutting out wicked and green with river slime. On she went, her crew watching breathlessly to see if she would come around and tack into the wind in time.

Yes, she would! No; no; yes! Half a dozen times in as many seconds the chances changed, but still she swept on.

Suddenly, with a bump that threw all four boys prone on the deck, she struck the pier and, as they lay half dazed, she slid up the inclined stone, greased as it was with slime, until the forward part of her underbody was clear out of the water and her stern deep in. With a jar the motion ceased, and then she began to slide backward. Deeper and deeper went her stern until it seemed as if she would dive backward.

At last she slid off altogether and, turned around into the wind by the impact with the pier, began to pay off on the other tack. Ransom jumped up and seized the tiller, amazed and delighted that the boat still held together and that he and his companions were uninjured.

The draw now commenced to swing again and Ransom, watching it over his shoulder, saw it open wider and wider until the channel was clear. Then he put the boat about again and she sailed calmly through the gap, Arthur at the main sheet, Clyde tending the jib and Frank forward as before.

A prolonged cheer rose from the men on the draw, and a faint shout came down the wind from the people on the other bridge. Cheer on, if the gallant little ship was not racked to pieces and strained beyond repair.

"Arthur, get below and sound the pump," said Ransom anxiously. The mate flew down the companionway, and the boys on deck soon heard the suction of the pump and the swish of the stream thrown in the center-board trunk. It was a time of suspense until the sucking sound was heard that betokened that she was dry. The good Michigan white oak held true; beyond some slackened stays and a broken turnbuckle, the yacht was uninjured.

"By George, boys!" exclaimed Arthur as he came from below. "She's the stuff! You can't hurt her. She's as sound as can be—not a seam started."

From here on, the Illinois was plain sailing. Wafted by favoring winds and a swift current, the *Gazelle* made fast time and reached the Mississippi on Thanksgiving Day.

"Boys," said Ransom, as he came up from examining the charts, "if we have luck today, we'll be sailing on the Mississippi."

" A mighty good way to celebrate the day," suggested the mate.

"I wonder what it looks like," Clyde speculated.

"Oh! I think it's very broad, and very muddy, with low banks covered with colored people singing songs to a banjo." This was Arthur's contribution.

"No, I think that we'll find the banks lined with wood piles, with here and there a plantation landing..."

"And boats, great flat-bottomed things," Frank interrupted Clyde to say, "with tall chimneys instead of stacks belching rolls of black smoke."

"You fellows have been reading Mark Twain and think you know it all," Kenneth remarked from his place at the tiller. "But where do you suppose we are now? Look around."

The boys had been so busy making up an imaginary river that they did not notice when they passed a low point and entered into what appeared to be a wider part of the stream.

"Why, you don't know the Mississippi when you see it! Let's give three cheers for it," cried the captain.

"Hip, hip, hurrah!" The cheers rang out together with a will.

"Now three more for the boat."

Again they rang out, undignified, perhaps, but fitting, in that they voiced the thanksgiving which all four of the crew felt but could not express in words.

As the sun sank, turning the brown waters of the mighty river to crimson and gold, the *Gazelle* dropped her anchor in a little cove and rested while her crew partook of mallard duck, shot during the day—their Thanksgiving dinner.

"People said we wouldn't be able to cross the lake safely, eh?" said Frank, exultantly. "And here we are, anchored to the bottom of the Mississippi. We're the people."

"Going to take on a pilot, Ken?" suggested Arthur.

"Sure!" returned the captain. "Who will give up his berth to him?"

"Oh, I guess we can get along without one," Arthur interposed hastily. "Clyde, give me some more duck."

"This mallard is all right, Clyde," remarked Kenneth rather thoughtfully. "But I confess I'd swap it for a homemade pumpkin pie."

"Now drop that, Ken," said Clyde. "I object to your invidious comparisons. It isn't a square deal to call to mind home feasts on Thanksgiving night anyway."

After dinner they all went on deck and looked for a long time on the mighty river, about which they had heard and read so much, but which none of them had seen before—the river that was to carry them to the salt water which, in spite of the 1,300 odd miles that lay between it and them, seemed nearer now that they were on the direct course. It appeared an easy thing for them to float down that great stream and let the current carry them down to the Gulf.

The four turned in, elated, a feeling tempered, however, by the thought that they were far from home, and were widening the distance between them and it at a rapidly increasing pace. Had they foreseen what was before them on this steadily flowing, almost quiet stream, they would have slept even less quietly.

Early morning saw them busy washing down decks, airing the bedding, etc., while a savory odor rose on the quiet air. As soon as this fragrance spread itself, it might be noticed that the crew accelerated their motions, the brooms and brushes were plied with greater zeal, the sails were raised to dry them with greater vigor, and, in fact, all the morning chores were hastened with telltale rapidity.

But before anyone got any breakfast—unless it was a surreptitious bite taken by the cook himself—the anchor was tripped, the jib hauled up, all the sails sheeted home and the run to St. Louis begun.

Sailing on the Mississippi seemed an easy thing. It was broad and deep and smooth. Indeed, the boys were congratulating themselves on the ease with which they had conquered the terrible "Father of Waters" Mississippi, when there was a crash in the cabin and a terrible bump from below. Frank jumped down the companionway with a single leap and found the center-board bobbing up and down in its trunk and the ship's best china cup lying in fragments on the floor. It had been resting on the top of the trunk when the center-board struck a sandbar, bobbed up and knocked the cup to flinders.

Their overconfidence was gone in a minute, and soon they were paying the customary tribute to that always uncertain stream—heaving the lead and taking soundings. The *Gazelle* got over the bar all right, but the lesson was not forgotten.

The second day after leaving the mouth of the Illinois River they passed under the great Eads Bridge and anchored a little below St. Louis.

"Who's going ashore?" Clyde looked around from one to the other of his companions. "I think it is our turn. The starboard watch ought to have a loaf once in a while, you know."

"Not by a jugful! Hasn't the port watch been at the helm all day?" Arthur was more vehement than it was necessary he should be.

"Well, we did all the dirty work, cooked the meals and washed the dishes." Frank was getting interested.

"Here, here, let's quit this squabbling. We all have worked hard and we all want to go ashore, and each has an equal right, but some of us must stay." Ransom realized that quarreling would spoil the trip quicker than anything else.

The three stood, in an attitude that said as plainly as words: "What are you going to do about it?"

"Leave it to these." Kenneth showed four ends of rope yarn sticking out of his closed hand. "These yarns are of different lengths. The two that get the shortest will have to stay aboard. The lucky two who pull the longest can go ashore. See?"

"It goes," the three answered.

The upshot of it was that Clyde and Frank went ashore, and the other two remained to keep ship and do chores.

It was late when the "liberty party" returned with pockets bulging with letters and papers, with heads full of the things they had seen and tongues aching to tell of them, and last, but not least, with able-bodied appetites and stomachs ready for the meal which the "left-behinders" had prepared.

It would be hard to tell whether the tongues or the knives and forks won the race, but certainly both did valiant service. By way of compensation, the starboarders washed the dishes while the port did the heavy looking-on. Soon things were cleared away and the hinged table was lined with boys reading letters.

"Look at this," said Kenneth, after a time of quiet broken only by the crackle of stiff paper. "I had hoped that this would show up about this time. We need it in our business."

It was a check for $125, and was expected to last them many weeks. The money that Kenneth had saved for this trip had been left in his father's hands, to be forwarded from time to time as needed, and almost every cent of the little hoard had its particular use.

"Well, don't be proud," exclaimed Arthur, "You are not the only one," and he flourished a money order.

Frank, too, produced one.

"We are bloated bondholders," the captain said, smiling. "But we won't spend it on riotous living now, or we'll have to eat and drink Mississippi River water later."

Arthur was under the weather next day, so Ransom went ashore alone, taking the precious check and money orders with him. He rather despaired of finding anyone who would identify him so that he could cash the check. But as luck would have it, he met an acquaintance on the street who made him all right with the bank officials at once.

John Brisbane was a pleasant fellow and knew the city thoroughly. He towed Ransom around the town and showed him most of the sights, and even introduced him to some Mississippi pilots. They listened to his tale of what he and the crew had done and intended still to do with polite incredulity for a while, but finally, concluding that he was telling them a "tall story," they began to jeer openly.

"That's right," Ransom protested earnestly, a little vexed but still smiling. "We are planning to go around the eastern United States, and we'll do it, too."

After the river men saw that he was in earnest and that he really intended to put the trip through, they began to tell him things about the river: where to look for this bar, how to avoid that eddy, and where deep water ran round the other bend. Indeed, they gave him so much information about the Mississippi between St. Louis and New Orleans that he was bewildered, and felt as if he were waking up from a dream wherein someone was reading a guidebook of the river, while another called off the soundings of the charts.

When he finally bid goodbye to the pilots, Ransom felt thankful to get away with his reason intact. Then John Brisbane showed him the post office and, after bidding him goodbye and good luck, went off.

Ransom found that he had barely time to cash his money orders and feared that when he got on the end of the long line in the crowded waiting room the window would be closed before he got to it.

One by one the people stepped up to the narrow window and held what seemed to be long conversations with the official behind the glass. First it was a woman with a baby, which had to be held by someone else while the mother signed her name, the baby meanwhile objecting vigorously; then a man with a lot of bundles, which he was constantly dropping and as often picking up, delayed the line; and then one thing after another until Ransom, who watched the hands of the big clock approach nearer and nearer four o'clock, fingered his money orders nervously and grew nearly frantic with apprehension.

At last he reached the window and got his money just in time. He put it in the inside pocket of his coat and buttoned it up, but pulled it open again when he went over to the stamp window to buy stamps for the crew and for himself. The crowd was unaccountably thick, and he wondered at it, as a man pushed against him so heavily that he grunted. The stamps bought, he rushed out to buy some greatly needed supplies for the ship's larder.

"It's lucky I got that money," he said to himself, as he opened the door of a grocery shop. "We would have about starved to death if it had not come."

"How much is it?" Ken asked the grocery man when the goods had been selected.

"Three forty-eight," was the reply.

Ransom went into his vest pocket, where he usually carried a small amount of money for everyday purposes, and pulled up two quarters, a nickel and two pennies. "Fifty-seven cents," he laughed, while the grocery man watched him narrowly.

"Well, it *is* lucky that check came. What we should have done without it, I don't know." He reached for his inside pocket as he spoke. "But it did, so it's all right. How much did you———"

He stopped in the middle of the sentence: the pocket was empty! He ran his hand way down in: empty. He turned the pocket inside out: not a thing in it. Then he felt each pocket in turn rapidly, then carefully—no money.

The grocery man began putting away the things which Kenneth had bought. Ransom did not notice him but kept up his frantic search with no result. He stopped to think. The perspiration stood in drops on his brow, and a leaden weight had settled down on his heart as he realized that he had been robbed of over a hundred dollars of his earnings, every cent of which was needed to carry him through. He felt sure that his pocket had been picked at the post office. Then the thought came to him with crushing force that he had lost the money of the other boys, and that he would have to make it up out of what was left of his small hoard at home.

"Perhaps I dropped it," he thought to himself, and he rushed back to the post office to see.

He searched the big room desperately, and was so evidently troubled that the watchman asked him what he was looking for.

"I lost some money here; have you seen anything of it? I will pay a reward."

The man looked at him incredulously, then laughed in his face. "Found any money? I guess not! Why, there's been a thousand people in this room today. Found any money? Just listen to that!" He broke into a laugh again and turned his back on the distracted boy.

Kenneth wandered aimlessly out into the corridor, every nerve racking with agony. As he walked along, he saw among a lot of names, titles of departments and courtrooms, "U.S. MARSHAL."

"I guess I'll ask him; he ought to know if there are pickpockets around here, and he may help me," and suiting the action to the word, Ransom made for the room.

The assistant marshal, a small, keen-eyed, albeit kindly man, was just closing the office when the boy burst in.

"I have lost some money," Ransom began right away. "Stolen out of my pocket, I think."

"When?"—the question came out like a pistol shot.

"This afternoon, when I——"

"Where?" the other interrupted in the same sharp way. He acted as if he was especially interested.

"Downstairs, in the money order and stamp room." Ransom was getting even more excited—the other's manner was catching.

"Describe it."

Ransom paused to think a minute, and then began slowly as the denominations of the bills came to him.

"One twenty, eight tens, four fives, two twos and a dollar bill. Then," and he paused again, "there was besides two fives and five twos and three fives."

As he spoke, the marshal began fingering the combination of the safe, his back to Kenneth, but the boy was so engrossed that he did not notice what he was doing.

"Well, you've got a good memory, youngster. Here's the money." With that the marshal turned and handed out a bunch of bills and some letters.

"What!" the boy exclaimed, amazed, his cheeks flushing and his breath coming in quick gasps as he dropped into a chair. "Oh!"

"Your name is Kenneth, you said?" The official was smiling. "Well, I am going to name my youngest Kenneth, so that he will always come out on top— I congratulate you."

He put out his hand and Kenneth, half dazed with his unexpected good fortune, grasped it with both of his. In his gratitude he felt the uselessness of words, and though he tried on all the different ones he could think of that would apply to the situation, not one of them seemed adequate.

"How did it happen?" his curiosity made him ask at last.

"Oh, I saw a fellow in a dark corner looking over something," the marshal explained, "and I just did not like his looks—he must have been a green hand to be looking at his graft in the open like that. So I went up to him and asked him if he had found something. The fellow looked up, saw my uniform and got a case of cold feet right away. 'Yes,' he said, half scared, 'I found this by the money order window.' All the same, he still held onto the wad—he hated to give it up—so I remarked, quiet like, 'I guess you found it in somebody's pocket.' Well, I got the roll quick enough then, and put it in the safe, but I never expected the owner would run it to earth as quickly as you did."

Kenneth thanked him again and gave him a bill from the roll which he was holding. The marshal finally had to cut off his torrent of thanks with a short "Young man, this office closed an hour ago."

Ransom from the door shouted an invitation to visit the yacht, and then went back to the grocery man and made him do up the things he had ordered before with elaborate care. He paid his $3.48 and went off, the most thankful boy in town.

A PERILOUS SITUATION

Though Kenneth was elated enough when he left the center of the city and started for the riverfront, his heart sank within him when he caught sight of the water. The swift current was carrying great pieces of ice, which gleamed white against the dark stream. The ice cakes were close together and, as the boy thought of the scant three-eighths of an inch thickness of *His Nibs*'s sides, he despaired of reaching the yacht anchored on the other shore.

"But what shall I do?" he asked himself. "The boys haven't any boat, and I've got the eatables."

It seemed hard that he should fall from one nerve-racking experience into another, with scarcely a breathing space between times.

For the next five minutes or so he studied the surface of the water, hoping that a time would come when the ice ran less thick; but he realized that each minute of waiting was precious daylight lost. Running down the sloping bank of the levee, he tumbled his bundles into the frail little boat, unmoored her and pushed out between two monster river steamboats.

For a minute he paused to pull himself together, saw that all was snug on board, settled his cap more firmly on his head and prepared for the struggle to come.

Then out from the shelter of the huge boats he shot—nerves tense, eyes alert. *His Nibs* was on its best behavior and obeyed its master's slightest touch, as if it understood the desperate situation. The rowboat was short and so could spin around like a top on occasion.

The river seemed bent on destroying the boy and his little craft. It hurled great chunks of sharp-edged ice at him in quick succession, but he always succeeded in dodging them somehow. Twisting this way and that, now up stream, now down, he made his way painstakingly over toward the *Gazelle*, lying so peacefully at anchor in the little cove near the other shore.

A warning shout told the three boys that the captain they were so anxious about was returning, and they rushed on deck to greet him. It was well they did so, for he had hardly strength enough to throw them *His Nibs*'s painter and climb aboard.

"Boys," said Ransom, after he had told of his adventures, "St. Louis is a nice city, but let's get out. It's hoodooed for me."

In spite of Ransom's determination to leave St. Louis at once, however, it was several days before the ice permitted them to move from their anchorage. Many friends had been made in the meantime and nothing unpleasant occurred, so it was with a feeling of regret rather than joy that the voyagers finally pulled up the mudhook and began in earnest the sail down the Mississippi.

The newspapers had found out that the *Gazelle* and her crew were in port, and many of the inhabitants knew about and were interested in the little craft and her youthful sailors.

The channel followed the city side of the river, and as the *Gazelle* got underway, the steamboats lining the levee, bow in, stern out, gave her a rousing salute on whistles of varying tones. People on deck waved their hands and shouted "Good luck!" and "Godspeed!"

The ice was still very much in evidence, and kept the steersman busy on the lookout, but Kenneth managed, in spite of that, to enjoy the attention which they received.

"St. Louis is not so bad a place, after all," he declared with a change of heart.

The ice gave the youngsters a great deal of trouble. It was necessary to keep on the watch continually, and to luff or tack every little while to avoid slamming into a jagged-edged piece. The channel was very crooked and crossed continually from one side of the stream to the other. The "Father of Waters" had a decided mind of his own, and no matter how carefully and laboriously a straight channel was dredged, he was quite likely to abandon it and make a new one.

The boys found the course a continual puzzle, and fairly gasped when they thought of the 1,200 miles of it still before them. But though the experience was trying, it was valuable, especially to Ransom, who learned just what a boat can do under numerous and ever-varying circumstances. It was the most intimate sort of experience, their very existence depending upon surmounting each difficulty in turn.

The first afternoon's run was 38 miles, which, considering the many delays on account of ice, the "crossings" and their unfamiliarity with the river's peculiarities, the boys thought very good. It was a rather trying sail, however, and all hands were glad when a snug little bend opened up, deep enough to give shelter to the yacht.

All four of the boys were by this time well-seasoned sailors. They had had some hard knocks, been through many close shaves, and knew what it was to be cold, hungry and tired. But as time went on they had become closer and closer friends. They learned to put up with each other's little peculiarities, and shook down into a harmonious ship's company. A cheerful atmosphere prevailed that promised final success and was an inspiration not only to themselves but to all who saw it. Their solid friendship was soon to be sorely tested—and proved—in a most unexpected manner.

Each had his special duties to perform, and as the voyage grew in length, each became more and more proficient. This was especially true of the cook, Clyde. Not that he was a poor one at the start, for he had shipped with the recommendation that in ten minutes he could cook a meal that the four could not eat in ten days. This was a little far-fetched, however, for the "rules and regulations" very plainly stated that anyone who could not satisfy his appetite in five hours would be obliged to wait until the next meal.

Nevertheless, the cook was very modest, and explained his improvement by saying that it was due to his becoming familiar with his quarters. In proof of this, he showed some pancakes which were not only round but also flat. In the beginning, owing to the listing of the vessel under the pressure of the wind on her sails, the batter would run to one side of the pan, and the pancakes had often been quite able to stand alone on end.

None of the boys could handle a needle very deftly at first, but they soon became very good seamsters. They even progressed so far in the art that they began to openly boast of their skills. Frank returned one night from a hunting trip ashore with a number of ducks and a shy look about him, which his companions were at a loss to account for until they discovered an unbecomingly large tear in his trousers. After supper he tackled the gap with a big needle and a couple of yards of linen thread. He wanted to have it good and strong, he explained.

Frank did not bother to take his trousers off, but began to sew the rent baseball-seam fashion, and though the result was not elegant as regards mere looks, he certainly accomplished his object, and he was justly proud of his achievement.

"Any of you fellows want any sewing done?" he remarked airily as he sawed off the end of the thread. "I am going to paint on the mainsail, in beautiful, gilt script letters, 'Monsieur Chauvet, Modes,' and rig you fellows up in natty sailor uniforms to ferry my customers over to me."

"Well, I don't know," Arthur remarked (he had been busy writing while Frank was embroidering); "I can sew (lo) a little, myself; listen."

He dodged a pillow, a spool, a ball of tarred twine and a book, and then began the following:

> *Gazelle, Gazelle,*
> She'll run pell-mell,
> With every stitch a-drawing,
> O'er waters smooth
> And waters rough,
> The seas her forefoot spurning.
>
> *Gazelle, Gazelle,*
> She's quite a swell;
> But yet there's no denying,
> If needs she must

Do it or bust
She'll be at anchor lying.

Gazelle, Gazelle,
You must do well,
On you depends our winning;
For 'tis our boast,
From lake to coast,
You'll bring us through a-spinning.

"For the sake of the song we'll forgive the pun, if you never let it occur again," said Ransom judicially.

It was late when they turned in that night, and Ransom was just on the verge of dozing off when he heard a great rustling in Frank's bunk across the cabin. Clyde and Arthur were asleep, so Ransom whispered, "What's the matter, old man?"

"Oh, Ken, I'm in trouble." There was a kind of gurgle in his voice that stilled the captain's anxiety. "If ever I get toploftical, you just pipe up a song about a fellow that sewed his outer clothes to his underclothes." Then followed a savage, ripping sound, which bespoke the tragedy, and all was still again.

. . . . .

In spite of their best efforts, it seemed as if the elements were against the young voyagers. One day a heavy mist fell, and made the following of the channel nothing more nor less than a game of blind man's buff, with the fun excluded, and a few sandbars, rocks and snags thrown in to make it interesting. Another day the snow fell so heavily that they had to tie up, the channel marks being obscured. Here they went ashore and visited the town of Herculaneum, a mining village, where Arthur and Kenneth took in the lead-smelting furnaces while Frank and Clyde stayed aboard.

Just before dark some river steamers passed and showed them the channel, and the boys gladly took advantage of their lead. The government dredges afforded Kenneth and his friends an opportunity to get acquainted with a new kind of craft, which the young ship designer was especially glad of. The government's dredging and snag-pulling boats are among the largest and most expensive in the world. It takes an endless amount of money and effort to harness the Mississippi, and the government is making a great fight to keep the river free of obstructions.

At Wittenberg, Missouri, where the boys tied up for a night, they got some much appreciated information from the usually taciturn river men about the Grand Tower Whirlpool. It was a spot which they had heard of way back in the Illinois River towns, as one of the most dangerous places on the old Mississippi.

It is the graveyard of many a fine river packet, and it can hardly be wondered at that our cruisers dreaded it greatly. A sharp bend in the river makes an eddy that has terrible suction power. To the left the water shoals rapidly; the bottom is covered with rocks, and is the resting place of snags, logs and all the debris that menace navigation.

Between this Scylla and Charybdis is the narrow channel. It is a spot to make even the experienced steamboat man think of his accident insurance policy, and it seemed almost madness for the young sailors, aided by the wind alone, to attempt to run the dangerous place.

The next morning dawned bright and clear. Half a gale was blowing straight downstream—that is, straight downstream when the river happened to flow north and south. Little whitecaps were puffed up from the brown flood, and streaks of ripples showed where the wind got a favorable slant. It looked squally, and it required all the resolution that the boys possessed to make the trial, the outcome of which would mean success or destruction. But they knew that indecision went hand in hand with failure, and they took their courage in both hands manfully and prepared for the ordeal.

"You can keep her going with a wind like this back of you," a new-found friend shouted as he cast off the line. "You'll have plenty of steerage way. Follow the marks and you're okay."

The last words grew fainter and fainter as the *Gazelle* fled away before the wind like a bird. Her motion was so swift, so sure, that the sailors she bore took heart and watched eagerly for the marks that would tell of their approach to the dread spot.

"There's the beacon," shouted Frank, who was on lookout duty forward.

Kenneth shifted the helm a little and bore nearer to shore.

"There's the other one," yelled Frank, "off our port bow."

Again the tiller was moved, this time a trifle to starboard.

The wind was blowing dead aft, almost a gale, and the *Gazelle* fled before it like a frightened thing. The speed of the current, too, increased. They were going like a race horse. Floating cakes of ice were left behind in a trice; the trees on shore flashed past like specters. It was a terrible pace.

They passed a point, and there, in the curve of the bend, the whirlpool seethed, a veritable cauldron of tumbling, foaming, riotous water. To the left the water was broken and frothy. The tough roots of uprooted trees reached out of the worried stream, and black rocks protruded like ugly teeth.

Between the two places of destruction ran a smooth, swift, straight channel, and for this the *Gazelle* headed like a well-aimed arrow. In an instant she was speeding through. To the right the whirlpool twisted and tossed; on the other side gaped the rock-toothed shoal. Straight on flew the boat, swifter and swifter, her crew quiet and steady, ready for whatever might come.

In a moment it was over, and the yacht was sailing smoothly on the comparatively still waters beyond.

"Good work, old girl!" Kenneth exclaimed half aloud. With each trial the boys had gained confidence in the boat until they had come to have an affection for her that made them wish there was some personal way of showing her their trust and regard.

The channel beyond Grand Tower was straight, deep and broad. The *Gazelle* bounded along, the breeze astern, at such a swift pace that she covered the 12 good miles to Devil's Island in one hour.

The crew were in high glee now and enjoyed every minute to the full; but, after all, they merely served to prove the truth of the proverb: "Pride goeth before a fall."

The water shoaled rapidly. All at once, without warning of any kind, the yacht stopped as if some giant's hand had grasped her keel and suddenly stayed her flight. Why it did not shake the masts off from her, the crew could never understand.

"Pull up the board, Clyde!" Kenneth shouted to that member of the company, who was below when the shock came. The boy picked himself up and pulled at the line which ran through a pulley made fast to the deck beams, and through a corresponding block on the center-board. He tugged and tugged, but the weight of the wind on the sails jammed the board in its trunk, and he could not move it.

The canvas was lowered and then the board came up. Arthur took *His Nibs* and an anchor, which he intended to drop overboard some distance from the yacht, when it would serve as a kedge to pull her over the obstruction, but before the mate got far enough to drop the hook, the sails, which had been raised meantime, caught the strong wind and hurried the yacht over the bar.

The *Gazelle* bounded forward.

"Heave over the anchor, Art!" Kenneth shouted as he jumped to the tiller. But the iron was so heavy and the speed of the yacht so great that the slack was taken in before the mate could obey the command. In an instant *His Nibs* was capsized and the mate was swimming around in the cold water in company with the cakes of ice. He soon found that the water reached only to his waist, however, and he waded quickly to *His Nibs*, bailed the boat out and paddled over to the *Gazelle*, which had meantime come up into the wind and was fast to the anchor dropped when the small boat capsized.

"Well," said Arthur as he scrambled aboard, "maybe I got excited, but I kept cool all right." He chuckled at his wit, though his teeth chattered suggestively and he had a blue look which his friends did not like to see. A sharp rubdown, a change of clothing and a cup of hot coffee brought him around in short order.

After this experience, luck seemed to be with the boys. They sailed down the wide river, crossing from side to side as the channel dictated, but with favoring winds and bright skies. The great stream was never monotonous, especially to the crew of a sailing craft. It was full of surprises and interests; its channel turned and twisted many times in a mile and changed every day.

But woe betide the vessel that depended on a misplaced beacon. It was this that nearly, so very nearly, ended the career of the *Gazelle* and her crew. At Goose Island, on the Missouri side, they ran aground, having laid their course according to a misplaced light.

It was a very serious situation which these youngsters had to face. The boat was caught hard and fast in a stream running from four to five miles an hour, carrying great chunks of ice that struck all obstacles with the force of battering rams. The bar was almost in midstream, too far away from shore to hail. A small boat of *His Nibs*'s strength would not live in the ice ten minutes. It was about as grim a predicament as could be imagined. All the sails were spread, the board raised, and the crew, with the exception of the man at the helm, shoved with oars for hours, but the *Gazelle* did not budge an inch.

Then they tried to take an anchor out, but *His Nibs* was no sooner put overboard than a big cake of ice came along and gave the light little craft such a terrific thump that the boys pulled her in hurriedly—they could not afford to run any risks with the only means they had of reaching shore.

Hour by hour the cold increased until it got close to the zero mark, and as the weather became colder the streams supplying the Mississippi froze up, and the water of the great stream grew less and less.

The boys worked with desperation, staying up late at night and rising at daybreak, hoping for a rise of water or a favorable slant of wind. The increased cold made it necessary to keep the oil stove burning, and the fuel began to get low. While sailing along the river, whose banks were lined with towns, the boys did not lay in a great stock of provisions; they thought it better to get them in fresh as frequently as possible.

"Well, Ken," Clyde remarked the third day of their imprisonment on the bar, "we will have to live on raw potatoes and river water pretty soon. My oil is about gone, and everything else is almost eaten up."

"There is one more thing to do," the captain said at length. "Throw out our pig iron ballast. I hate to lose it, but it is the only thing left to do.

All of the boys showed the effects of tremendously hard work, of the fight with cold and ice, with wind and water, but Kenneth was particularly worn. On him fell the responsibility. The others were in his care, and if anything happened to them, he knew he would be held accountable.

The constant strain, the lack of sleep—he was up all hours of the night— and his anxiety told on even his rugged health. He grew perceptibly thinner in three days, dark rings showed under his eyes and little things vexed him unwarrantably. They were all irritable, and it spoke well for their closely knit friendship that no words arose between them.

"Well, boys," Kenneth said, cheerfully enough, "let's play our last card. Let's turn to and throw over the ballast."

It was hard work lugging the heavy sash weights that made up the ballast from below and throwing them over the side. There was at least half a ton to be discarded, and by the time the last of it was overboard, the boys thought that there must have been tons.

Guess, then, how their hearts leaped with joy when at last, after three weary days, the *Gazelle* floated over the bar and into deeper water. But their triumph was short-lived, for they speedily found that there was another bar across the channel. The low water almost bared it, and they realized that they were trapped in a little basin a half-mile from shore, with absolutely no protection from the ice, which was running heavier and heavier.

To anchor and wait, trusting to Providence, was all they could do. So two anchors were dropped, and the boys faced the situation. The weather continued, piercing cold. The oil gave out altogether, and then the crew had to live on cold things and exist as best they could in the cold cabin.

The strain was even harder to bear than the cold and hunger. Great chunks of ice came sailing down on them continually, and the boys wondered each time if the *Gazelle* would be able to stand another such hard knock.

The bar beyond caught the majority of the larger chunks, and soon an ice gorge was formed that hourly grew bigger until the *Gazelle*'s stern was not 20 yards from it. Each new cake added to the heap and formed new teeth, which were ever moving in the rushing current—teeth which could grind up any living thing in a very few moments.

The second night after the *Gazelle* got afloat, the boys were in the cabin and all but Kenneth had fallen asleep from sheer exhaustion, the recurring bumps of drifting cakes of ice not disturbing them in the least. But Ransom could not sleep. He could not forget the horrible danger which they were in, nor could he shut his ears to the sound of crunching ice just behind the yacht.

Of a sudden there came a jar with a new quality in it. Ransom rushed up the companionway, grabbing his woolen cap as he ran, then forward over the ice deck. He found the ragged, frayed end of the anchor cable hanging overboard. The constant rubbing of the ice had weakened it and the extra heavy floe had completely sundered it. There was but one anchor now to depend on; if that should fail them, it would mean instant destruction to the yacht and certain death for her crew.

It was too great a risk to run—that other anchor must be found somehow and its holding power made good again.

Realizing that his companions would try to deter him from the desperate undertaking which he had in mind, Ransom did not call his friends, but quietly launched *His Nibs* from the stern, despite the current and the remorseless ice. Drawing her forward by the painter, he got in at the bow and prepared to feel for the parted anchor cable with a boat hook. He pulled hand over hand on the cable of the other anchor, and finally gained a point where he thought he might begin to reach for the sunken line.

It was well past midnight, and so dark that everything had to be done by sense of touch only. Intensely cold, the oars, the line he was holding and the boat hook—everything, in fact, was coated with a slippery skin of ice.

Holding on by one hand to the anchor cable and the other on the boat hook, Kenneth began to grope for the other line. His right arm ached with the exertion of feeling on the bottom with a heavy boat hook, while his left wrist seemed about to break with the strain put upon it. The cold nipped at his exposed face and wet, mittened hands, but still he persevered.

At last he felt the touch of the line at the end of his pole; he began to haul in slowly, holding the pole with his elbow as he took a fresh hold further up. Suddenly a huge floe struck the little boat, dragging the anchor line out of his grasp, and pulling him backwards into the bottom of the boat. The current swept him back, past the *Gazelle* and on toward the gnashing teeth of the gorge.

AN ARCTIC ADVENTURE

"Arthur! Clyde! Frank! O-o-o-oh, boys!" It was a despairing cry that rang over those dismal, freezing waters. "Help!"

It was too late—no help from the *Gazelle* could save the boy in his frail craft. The current had swept him beyond the reach of anyone on board, even if a soul had been awake to hear his call for help. The grinding, crushing, gnashing sounds of the crumbling ice on the gorge grew nearer and nearer.

Kenneth scrambled to a sitting position and searched with groping hands in the darkness for the oars. At last he found them—no, only one. A misplaced brace deceived him.

Again he searched with desperate haste. He could hear the lap of the water on the piled-up floes now. The other oar was not there; he dimly remembered now that he dropped it when he fell backward.

Putting out his one oar, he began to scull with it, but the boat had drifted around, broadside to the current, and he could not head it away from the inexorable wall of ice now so close. At last he gave the struggle up and trusted to Providence. He comprehended how puny and futile his own strength was, compared to the power of these mighty odds.

The boat drifted nearer and nearer to what seemed certain destruction. Ransom crouched low, prepared to spring to any cake that might bear his weight—it was his only chance. He grasped the painter of the boat in his hand, and as soon as he felt the first bump of the broken ice against *His Nibs*'s side, he sprang at a white surface that showed dimly before him. By some lucky chance, or rather, owing to a merciful God, it was a large floe which, though it tottered and tipped dangerously, did not capsize. It bore the boy's weight bravely.

For a minute Kenneth paused for breath, when he noticed that *His Nibs* was being battered and ground by the constant action of the ice. He peered into the darkness to see how large his floating island was, and stepped cautiously this way and that to test its stability. It swayed frightfully, but the boy determined to risk adding the extra weight of the small boat. Inch by inch he drew it over the slippery surface, and deeper and deeper sank the ice island on that side until it was submerged half a foot or so.

Kenneth stood on the sharply inclined, slippery ice in imminent danger of sliding off. Though the temperature hovered around zero degrees, the perspiration stood out on his forehead in beads and ran into his eyes till it blinded him. Gradually *His Nibs* was hauled up until it rested beside him, for the time, at least, secure.

For a space he rested his aching limbs and bruised back. The white shape of the *Gazelle* could be faintly made out through the gloom, so near and yet absolutely unattainable. Never before had the boy—the designer, builder and owner of the craft—so yearned for her. She was cold, cheerless and in extreme peril herself, but she seemed a very haven of rest and security to the castaway.

Kenneth realized that he must fight for his own life and that no aid would be forthcoming from the yacht, and he began to study the situation. Grim enough he found it. A strong current bore down on the gorge, carrying ice and debris of every kind, grinding away at the edge of Ransom's floe. It was evident that it would break up eventually, and the boy prayed that it would last until he should find some other refuge.

He noticed that bits of wood and fragments of ice floated off to the right after colliding with the obstruction. This set him to thinking. There must be some break through that caused the current to swerve. He looked long and intently to the right, but could make out nothing in the darkness. He felt sure, however, that there must be a channel somewhere, and he was determined to find it.

With great and laborious care he launched the boat and sprang into it. Fending off from the teeth of the gorge with his oar, he worked his way gradually to the right. Twice he had to jump to a floe and haul his boat out from between two grinding cakes. But in spite of the labor, of darkness, of weary limbs and hands numbed with cold, he gained, until at last he reached the gap and was carried through.

He floated nearly a mile before he could make his way to shore. It was bleak enough, but he uttered a fervent "Thank God" as he set foot on solid ground.

The river bordered a cornfield at this point, and many of the rotting stacks were still standing. Kenneth made for one of these and, burrowing into it, sank down to rest. He was desperately weary and almost unbearably cold, but thankful to his heart's core for his escape.

"If I could only rest here till morning," he thought. It was a sheltered spot, and he began to feel the reaction following his tremendous exertions. He was languid and drowsy, and his fast stiffening muscles cried out for rest. It was a temptation the sorely tried boy found hard to resist, but the thought of his friends aboard the yacht, their state of mind when they discovered his absence and the loss of their only means of reaching shore urged him on and gave him no peace. His imagination pictured the hazardous things the boys might do if he were not there to calm them.

As he lay curled upon the frozen ground under the stiflingly dusty stalks, visions arose of the boys jumping overboard and attempting to swim ashore; of their setting the *Gazelle* adrift in the hope that she would reach the bank. Many other waking dreams disturbed him, most of them absolutely impracticable, but to his overtired and excited imagination painfully real, and his anxiety finally drove him out of his nest into the biting cold again.

Then Kenneth stopped to think, to plan a minute. He had but one oar—he could not row against the strong current and floating ice—he could not drag the boat through the water; the shore was too uneven and fringed, moreover, with ice. Bare fields and brown waters surrounded him, there was no sign of human habitation, there was no help to be had, and he must reach the yacht that night—but how? He studied hard and could think of but one way: to drag *His Nibs* overland until he was above the *Gazelle*'s anchorage, then launch it and drift down with the current.

How great the distance was he did not know, but he realized that it was a long way and that the journey could only be made by the hardest kind of work, under the most trying of circumstances.

His very body revolted at the cruelly hard exertions, every nerve and muscle crying for rest, but his will was strong, and he forced his aching body to do his bidding.

His Nibs weighed but 75 pounds with her entire equipment, but what the boat lacked in *avoirdupois* it gained twofold in bulkiness. There was some snow on the ground, and this helped somewhat to slide the small craft along on its strange overland journey.

So began the hardest experience Ransom had ever yet encountered. Facing the stiff wind and zero temperature, he slowly dragged the dead weight over the thinly frosted ground. Oh, so slowly he crawled along; now going around an obstruction, now climbing over a stump—forever hauling the reluctant boat along. Every few hundred yards the nearly exhausted lad stopped to catch his breath and rest under a heap of cornstalks or a mound of rubbish, burrowing like an animal. His hands and feet ached with cold. Several times his ears lost their sense of feeling and had to be rubbed back to life with snow.

He grew dizzy with faintness, for it will be remembered that he and the other boys had had insufficient food for days, and he had not eaten a morsel since six o'clock. His back ached, his head ached, he was utterly exhausted; but still he kept on doggedly.

At last he reached a point on a line with the *Gazelle*; he could just make her out silhouetted against the sombre sky. He knew his journey was nearly at an end, and he pushed forward with a last desperate gathering together of his powers.

At length, judging that he was far enough up stream to launch, he shoved *His Nibs*'s stern into the water with fear and trembling, for the little craft had passed through a trying ordeal, scraping over rough ground, stones and sticks. Ransom could not see if the frail craft leaked, but it certainly floated. He jumped in and pushed off, still anxious but hopeful, feeling that he was homeward bound. The *Gazelle* was still afloat—the thought cheered him.

With the single oar in hand he sat in the stern sheets, and using it as both a rudder and a propeller, he avoided some floes and lessened the shock of contact with others. At last the *Gazelle* loomed up ahead, serene and steady—the dearest spot on earth to the castaway.

"All right, boys," Kenneth shouted huskily as he drew near, "I'm okay."

There was no response.

His Nibs swept alongside and Kenneth, grasping at the shrouds, stopped himself and clambered stiffly aboard. All was quiet. His imagination pictured all sorts of horrible mishaps to the crew, and he ran aft, stopping only to secure *His Nibs*. Yanking open the frosted hatch, he pulled open the door and rushed below.

A chorus of snores greeted him. Not one of them knew he had been gone four hours.

Kenneth did not disturb them, but after hauling the small boat on deck out of harm's way he crawled into his bunk and fell into the stupor of utter exhaustion.

Early next morning all hands were wakened by the bump and crash of ice, and another day of anxiety began. The morning after, however, found an improvement in the conditions—the ice had almost stopped running and the weather moderated. *His Nibs* was launched and the bottom was sounded for half a mile in every direction in hopes that a channel might be found to shore or down the river to a more sheltered spot.

But bars obstructed everywhere. There was no water deep enough to float the yacht at her present draft, except in the basin in which she rested.

"Well, here goes the rest of our ballast," said Ransom after the last soundings had been taken; and all hands began with what strength they had left to heave over the iron. By taking down the rigging and tying it together, it was found that a line could be made fast to shore. The sturdy little anchor was raised and the *Gazelle*, working her windlass, was drawn to the bank. In her lightened condition she floated over the bars. Once more they were safe, and the boys felt that God had been good to them to bring them through so many perils.

Frank, the nimrod of the party, went ashore and shot a rabbit. A fire was built and soon all hands were feasting on hot, nourishing food—the first in many days. How good it tasted only those who have been nearly starved can realize.

The sleep which the four voyagers put in the night of the 12th of December, 1898, was like that of hibernating bears, and fully as restful.

Kenneth and Arthur drew the long strands of yarn this time, and set off to find Commerce, Missouri, ten miles across country. It was a long walk, but the two boys enjoyed it hugely—indeed, it was a relief to be able to walk straight ahead without having to stop to turn at the end of a cockpit or the butt of a bowsprit.

For the first few miles the talk was continuous, and many were the jokes about the mockery of the phrase "the Sunny South" when the mercury lingered about the zero mark. But as they neared the end of their journey they talked less and put more of their strength into the unaccustomed exercise of walking.

Reaching the town, they telegraphed home that all was well— a message which they knew would relieve much anxiety. They also wrote to the postmasters along the line to send mail to the crew at Commerce. Then, for the first time in two months, they slept in a bed—a luxury they felt they fully deserved.

The boarding house at which they had put up was a clean, pleasant place, and the bed, the feather variety, seemed veritably heaven to them. Two pleasant girls were also staying at this house, and the boys had the added pleasure of feminine society. They talked to the interested maidens of their adventures until the girls' faces flushed and their eyes brightened—yes, and moistened, even—with sympathy when they were told of an especially trying experience.

They had had many interested listeners all along the line, but the hero-worshipping looks in the eyes of the two girls was particularly sweet to the boys.

"Say, Ken," Arthur said comfortably, as he tumbled into bed, "let's stay a week."

"Yes, this bed is immense, isn't it?"

"Oh, hang the bed!" Arthur growled. "You're the most material duffer; there is something besides creature comforts in this world, after all, you know."

"No, I am not. I appreciate a pretty audience as much as"— Ransom interrupted himself with a yawn—"you do, but whaz-zer use of discussing——"

Another yawn stopped his speech, and at the end of it he was sound asleep.

"H'm!" grunted Arthur in disgust, and he turned his back upon him.

The purchases the two made the next day weighted their backs but lightened their pockets, and Ransom had to telegraph for more money. It took considerable resolution to break away from the pleasant society at the boarding house and trudge the long miles to the yawl carrying a heavy pack, but they summoned up courage and, with a pleasant goodbye and a grateful "come again" ringing in their ears, they once more started out on their adventures.

At the end of three days they were back again, Kenneth to receive his money order, which was due by that time, and the mate to help carry more supplies. That night they told more thrilling tales and took part in a candy-pull. The next day Arthur had to return alone. Kenneth's money order had not come, so he had to wait for it.

"Why didn't I work the money order racket?" said Arthur as he reluctantly shouldered his pack. "Ransom's in luck this time."

For a week Kenneth waited for word from home. Then he began to get nervous; he did not know if all was well or not. Letters came for the other boys, but none for him. He got more than nervous; he became absolutely anxious. Moreover, he wanted to get underway again. The little town of Commerce, with its 1,600 people, he had explored thoroughly; made excursions into the woods and had some good shooting; but in spite of unaccustomed pleasures he was restless. He wanted to be moving down the river again.

Whether it was the lack of news from home or some other cause, he could not tell, but he had a foreboding of some impending disaster. At the end of the sixth day of his stay in the little Missouri town, Frank appeared. An anxious look was on his face.

"My! I'm glad to see you, Ken," said he. "We wondered what

had become of you, so I traipsed over to see."

Kenneth explained the difficulty. "Everything all right aboard the *Gazelle*?" he asked.

"Well, no," Frank said reluctantly. "When are you coming back?"

"Tomorrow, I hope. But what's the matter aboard?" Kenneth remembered his forebodings. "Don't keep me waiting; what is it?"

"The fact is, Arthur's sick, and neither Clyde nor I know what to do for him."

"What's the matter with him?"

"I don't know. He has a bad cold and some fever, I guess, and he seems kind of flighty." Frank began to reveal his anxiety. "When he showed up the other day after walking from here he talked sort of queer about the game you played on him, the girls you met and about a feather bed—got 'em all mixed up. Had a terrible cough, too. He's in bed now."

"I wish I could go back with you, but I will have to wait for that money—I need it."

Frank returned alone after taking a good rest, and Ransom waited for news from home.

Late in the afternoon of the next day it came. Cheerful, helpful letters from the dear ones in Michigan. The money order came, too.

Kenneth bought his supplies and, after bidding his friends goodbye, started out on the long journey. During his stay in Commerce the weather had softened, the frost had come out of the ground and thick, sticky mud made walking difficult. The boy stepped out in lively fashion, in spite of the 85-pound pack he carried and the heavy rubber boots he wore. He forgot the weight and discomfort in his anxiety to get to the yacht and the sick friend aboard her.

It was four o'clock when he started, and he had not been on his way much over an hour before the darkness fell, and he had to pick his way warily. Of necessity he moved slowly, and the pack grew heavier with every stride. The sticky mud held on to his rubber boots so that his heels slipped up and down inside until they began to chafe and grow tender.

An hour later he was still walking—more and more slowly under the weight of the pack, which seemed to have acquired the weight of a house. Blisters had formed on his heels and were rapidly wearing off to raw flesh.

When he hailed the *Gazelle* at seven o'clock after three hours of most agonizing trudging, he was very nearly exhausted and his heels were bleeding. The absolute necessity of reaching Arthur soon and of applying the little knowledge he had of medicines had kept him from going under and given him courage to go on his way.

"Thank God, you've come!" was Clyde's greeting when he came to ferry Kenneth over.

"How's Arthur?" was the skipper's first inquiry.

"Crazy, clean crazy, and awful sick." Clyde was clearly greatly worried.

"Oh! I guess he'll come out all right."" Ransom saw that it was his play to put on a cheerful front and conceal the anxiety, the physical weariness and pain he felt. "You can't kill a Morrow, you know."

They stepped aboard and the first thing the captain heard was his friend's incoherent muttering.

Arthur lay tossing on his bunk in the chilly, musty cabin, half-clothed and in very evident discomfort. His eyes were open and it cut Kenneth to the quick to see that there was not a sign of recognition in them.

All weariness and pain were forgotten in the work which followed to make the sick boy more comfortable. Hot soups were prepared and fed to him. Ransom had luckily provided a medicine chest for just such an emergency, and now he drew on its resources wisely.

It was midnight before Arthur was quieted and asleep. During the entire evening the three boys were as busy as they could be, cooking, heating water, cleaning up and setting things to rights. Then only could a council be held and the situation discussed in all its bearings.

"Well, Doc," said Frank, smiling wanly, "What do you think is the matter with Art?"

"I wish I was an M.D." No wish was more fervently spoken. "Oh, Arthur has a bad cold, I think," Ransom began his diagnosis, "and his nerves are used up. Too much ice pounding and threatening, and not enough sleep."

"What shall we do?" Clyde asked. "These are pretty small quarters to care for a sick man."

"We'll spoil his rest cluttering around," suggested Frank.

"Well, I think that if we put him ashore in a hospital he would miss us and the familiar things around; he would have nothing to think of but himself, and he would worry worse," Kenneth expressed his convictions with emphasis.

"But he would get better care," Frank objected.

"Oh, I think we can look out for him all right," the skipper interposed, "and I honestly believe that if he came to himself in a hospital with strange people around, nurses and things, he would think that he was terribly sick and the thought of it might really do him up. If we keep him aboard—and I promise you that I will nurse him with all-fired care," (Kenneth spoke so earnestly that his friends were touched and reached forth hands of fellowship) "I think that when he comes to and finds himself with us and on the old *Gazelle*, he will pull himself together in great shape and brace up. As long as Arthur has his nerve with him, he's all right. We have had a tough time of it, and he has lost his grip a bit, but I am dead sure that if we stick by him he will pull through all right."

"It's all right, old man," Clyde said heartily. "We are with you. Ain't we, Frank?"

Frank said nothing but got up and, crossing the cabin, took the skipper's right hand while Clyde took the left. The three gripped hard for a second in silence. It was a compact to stand together through the trials that they knew were coming.

It was a strange scene: the little cabin, dimly lighted by the swinging lamp; the sick boy in the corner bunk forward on the starboard side lay breathing heavily, his flushed face in deep shadow. The three boys sat on Ransom's bunk in a row on the opposite side, the soft light shining on their anxious faces, their hands still clasped.

Outside the great river rushed and the *Gazelle* tugged at her moorings, the rudder slatted, the booms creaked against the masts and the rigging hummed an answer to each passing gust.

It was a time to try the temper of the young voyagers, and bravely they stood the test.

"Well, what's the matter with turning in?" It was Kenneth's voice that broke the stillness.

Not till Frank and Clyde had begun to snore had Ransom time to care for his aching heels. To pull off his boots was trying, but when he came to take off his stockings he could hardly suppress a cry of agony. The blood had clotted and stuck to the raw spot, and it felt as if he was pulling the nerves out by the roots. It was a long time before the burning pain allowed him to sleep.

At the first opportunity the voyage was continued, and it was with a feeling of relief almost amounting to hilarity that the line ashore was cast off, and the *Gazelle*, her bowsprit pointing downstream, got underway again. That treacherous place, fraught with so many perils, such weariness, pain and anxiety, was behind them at last.

They were headed for the land of promise, the real "Sunny South."

Even Arthur seemed to be less fretful, less exacting. Perhaps the swish of the water along the yacht's smooth sides was soothing, or maybe the heave of the little craft as she felt the pressure of the wind comforted the sick boy. Certainly it had that effect on his more fortunate companions.

When the *Gazelle* flew past the mouth of the Ohio River and anchored just below, the crew felt that they were really getting there. They visited Cairo, and though they were impressed with the advantage of its superior location at the junction of the two great rivers, they were glad that they did not live in its low-lying streets.

At Columbus, Kentucky, the crew made the acquaintance of a physician and dentist who travelled about the south in a private car. Though Kenneth felt that his diagnosis of Arthur's case was correct, he was mighty glad to have a physician confirm it.

Arthur improved slowly—too slowly. He had a genuine case of nervous prostration. At times he was delirious, and then he lived over again all the horror of the yacht's long imprisonment in the drifting ice. The poor boy's malady made him exasperatingly irritable and hard to please, so that the cabin of the *Gazelle* was by no means the cheery home it had been.

But the captain's cheerful fortitude and determination to see the thing through in spite of hostile elements, scant means, sickness and utter ignorance of the stream inspired the busy members of the crew so that they worked together in beautiful harmony.

On the afternoon of Christmas Day the *Gazelle* drew abreast of the front of Columbus, Kentucky, and while Frank and Clyde went ashore for mail, Kenneth stayed aboard to look after the invalid mate and cook the Christmas dinner. As the fragrant odor of broiling game and steaming coffee rose, Kenneth thought of the faraway Michigan home; of his father, mother and relatives gathered around the ample, homey table; of the snatches of cheerful talk and gentle raillery; of the warmth and comfort and love.

"Say, Ken," sounded a plaintive voice from the other side of the cabin, "where are the boys? What are we waiting here for? Give me a drink, will you?"

It was a painful awakening, but Ransom satisfied Arthur's wants, soothed him, and braced himself with the determination that win he must, and win he would in spite of all obstacles.

SAILING WITH FROZEN RIGGING

From Columbus, Kentucky, to Memphis, Tennessee, as the crow flies is approximately 125 miles, but by river it is 228 tortuous, puzzling miles. This distance the *Gazelle* made in nine days, including delays caused by fog, adverse winds and extra careful sailing on account of the sick boy.

The party found the "Father of Waters" to be an absorbingly interesting stream. At every turn (and on an average there was a turn about every other minute, it seemed to them) they saw something new, something strange and interesting. As they cruised along, people told them of river towns which the Mississippi had not left far inland as it had gradually formed a new channel and straightened its course. Others told of farms which had contributed a third or even four-fifths of their acreage in a single year to the undermining current of the stream, the land not infrequently being added to another farm not far below.

The changes in the stream played all sorts of pranks with the boundaries of states. A man living in Missouri might in a single night find his property switched over into Kentucky or Tennessee, the boundary line, the Mississippi, having carved for itself a new channel and cut its way through a bend.

After leaving Columbus, Kentucky, the *Gazelle* found herself on a straight piece of water with a strong wind on the starboard quarter. Ransom claimed that every point of sailing was the

Gazelle's best—running, reaching and beating to windward, all best—but, at any rate, she skimmed along this day like a bird. Kenneth was at the stick, while Frank held the Mississippi guide to watch out for beacons and channel marks.

For once all was clear, the channel straight and no dangerous shoals marked. It was a relief to strike such a good piece of river. The air was bracingly cold and all three boys felt exhilarated.

"How is it down below, Art?" Frank inquired cheerfully. "How is it with the 'landlubber lying down below'?"

"I'm below, all right." The voice was weak but vehement. "Still, I object to being called a landlubber. I'll show you fellows one of these days that I'm as good a sailor as any of you."

"Art is getting touchy," said Kenneth. "He'll be all right soon, I am willing to bet."

"Will you look at that!" exclaimed Clyde, who had been gazing forward for some time. "Just wait until I get my gun."

He pointed to a black object that was bobbing up and down in the brown flood. It looked like an animal swimming against the strong current. While Clyde went below, Ransom shifted his helm in order to get nearer, and before he realized it they were bearing down on the object at terrific speed. The yacht, going with the current, was making almost ten miles an hour.

"Sheer off, for heaven's sake, Ken!" sang out Frank. "Quick!" Then as the yacht passed to starboard she passed the black thing which had excited Clyde's hunting instincts.

"Gee! You ought to know a 'sawyer' when you see it, by this time." Frank's tone was full of superior disgust.

"How did you find out what a sawyer was, Mr. Smarty?" Clyde was trying to conceal his gun behind him, and he looked foolish. "What is it, anyway? I bet you don't know."

"Don't I, just! It's a piece of timber, one end of which, water-logged, sinks to the bottom and is partly buried; the current overcomes the buoyancy of the wood from time to time and causes the upper end to sink. This makes the motion like a man sawing wood—hence the name."

"Thanks, Professor." Clyde made a mock bow. "But all the same, the captain himself didn't know what it was, and pretty near punched the boat's bottom full of holes.

As they went southward, the character of the country changed. The high, heavily timbered bluffs, often bold with jutting rocks, so characteristic of the upper river, began to give way to more easy slopes. The stream broadened and the level rose higher each day. Often, as the *Gazelle* sped along, a river steamer was met ploughing along up the great stream. Her long gangways raised up before her like horns (long gangways made necessary by the gently sloping banks and absence of docks). Her tall stacks, side by side, running athwartships, bore between them the insignia of the line, an anchor or a wheel. The stacks ended in a fancy top, which Ransom said reminded him of pictures of the trimming that little girls of long ago wore around the end of their pantalettes.

The river boats are very shallow, and very wide for their length, but in spite of their un-boatlike appearance and their great thrashing wheels, they make good time. Sometimes a speed of 15 miles an hour against the current, and 25 with the stream, is attained.

Kenneth congratulated himself repeatedly that he had started on this trip, for he realized that in no other way could he have gained so much information about shipping.

They stopped several days at Memphis, partly to give Arthur a quiet rest, partly because the weather conditions were against them.

At the levee a number of boats were nosing the bank, their long gangplanks outstretched before them like great arms. A constant stream of roustabouts trundling bales of cotton, rolling barrels, lugging boxes, went up the gangways. The mate stood near at hand, in a conspicuous spot where he could see and be seen, and so belabored the toiling men with torrents of words, that it seemed as if he was the motive power of the entire procession. The Negroes seemed not to notice him at all, but moved along at a steady, rhythmic gait.

Frank and Clyde stood watching. They marvelled at the amount of stuff carried aboard. "I bet they work the same racket that the spectacular shows employ," Clyde said after a while. "If you look aft there somewhere, you would see the same people carrying the same bundles and things ashore again."

"Oh, come off!" exclaimed the other.

"Yes, sure; they form an endless chain."

Frank vouchsafed him no further reply, but suggested that they try to get on board and see for themselves.

"Can we come aboard?" Frank shouted to the mate when he stopped to take breath.

"I reckon you can," was the answer. "Look out, you yellow-livered son of a bale of cotton! Do you want to knock the young gentlemen overboard?"

The two boys got on deck and out of range of the mate's rapid fire of invectives as soon as they could. As luck would have it, they ran up against a pilot the first thing, to whom they told something of their trip. From the hold, which was hardly seven feet deep, to the hurricane deck and the pilot house they went. The wheel house reached, the pilot was in his own domain, and he made them sit down while he pumped them dry. He marveled that a boat of the *Gazelle*'s draught could come through at this stage of the water with only sails for power.

From the great, brass-bound steering wheel to the tall boilers, which could not find room in the hold and showed half their circumference above the first deck, the boat was full of interest to the young voyagers.

"Jiminy! What a lot she carries," Clyde exclaimed as he noticed the pile of cotton bales, boxes and barrels, which was rapidly growing until it seemed as if it would fill the boat from her blunt bow to stern post.

"She'll carry a thousand tons without turning a hair," said the pilot calmly as he shook their hands. "Tell your captain to come aboard if he cares to."

Ransom did care to, and he went over the craft from keel to flagstaff, noticed her construction and marveled at her shallow-ness—it was part of his business as well as his pleasure, and he wondered how the steamboat mate's talk would sound if the oaths were left out. He imagined it would simply be intermittent silence.

In describing it afterwards, he said that the mate's language was like a rapid-fire gun with a plentiful supply of blank ammunition.

Arthur improved rapidly, and by the time they had explored Memphis—visited its fine old Southern mansions, the busy cotton market, and hobnobbed with the steamboat people—he seemed much more like his old self, though his painful thinness and weakness showed how seriously ill he had been.

After staying at Memphis for ten days, the *Gazelle* spread her sails and slipped down the river on her way to the sea.

At Peters, Arkansas, the boys spied a cabin boat tied up in a little cove, with a big "26" painted on its side.

"Well, this is luck!" said Kenneth. "There are the chaps we saw above Philadelphia Point. Hail them, Frank."

"Hulloo, *Twenty-six*!" Frank's shout rang out in the frosty air. "Is the boss in?"

A head appeared at the door of the cabin. "The boss is in, who wants to see him?" it said.

The *Gazelle* rounded to and tied up to the bank a little below the cabin boat. As soon as the sails were furled and everything made shipshape, all four boys visited their friends and, for the greater part of a week, spent most of their time aboard the roomy, warm houseboat. Arthur improved wonderfully and all hands began to gain weight and grow fit on the game which they shot.

The crew of the *Gazelle* were almost won over from the more strenuous life of sailing to the free and easy cabin-boat life, which is the nearest approach to tramping that a dweller on the water can come to. All along the river the boys saw cabin boats drifting slowly along downstream, or tied up in the shelter of little coves near some town. Boats of varying degrees of respectability composed this fleet. Boats well built, clean and always brightly painted, homes of fairly prosperous families, whose head worked on shore while the home was afloat, in such manner saving rent and taxes. Boats built of bits of timber, boards and rusty tin, shanties afloat, the temporary homes of the lowest order of river people.

Theaters, dance halls, dives of various sorts, churches, stores— all had their representatives on the mighty stream. A great host of nomadic people followed the heat to lower river in winter and ran upstream from it in summer. Many of the river people were like the dwellers of number 26, merely temporary members of the river community who took this method of seeing the river, resting from the stress of business.

It was with a feeling of regret that the boys at last took leave of their hosts and went aboard their thoroughly cleaned and freshened yacht. All hoped that the "goodbye" they shouted over the fast-widening strip of water would prove after all to be only "au revoir."

"There's no use talking, boys," the skipper said gravely. "We've just got to hump ourselves and get south, where it's warm, so that we won't have to burn so much oil. It's simply ruinous."

"All right. If you keep healthy, Art, and we don't run aground and the boat don't get holes punched in her with the ice," Clyde remarked, "we may see New Orleans before the glorious Fourth."

"It's no joke, Clyde," said Ransom. "I'm almost busted, and I won't have enough to carry me through the Gulf if we don't hurry."

"Like the old gent who hurried up to finish his job before his whitewash gave out," laughed Frank.

But in spite of good resolutions and ardent hopes, progress was slow. Headwinds sprang up, dense fog shut down, obscuring channel marks—even snow fell. The weather was certainly against them.

"The 'Sunny South,'" Ransom quoted scornfully one morning when he put his head out of the companionway and got a block of snow down his neck. "They have a funny brand of sun down here." Yet as he looked shoreward, his eye rested on an old southern mansion. Fluted columns supported its double portico; wide-spreading trees from which hung in festoons the (to northern eyes) weird Spanish moss, clustered thickly about. Beyond were cotton fields, the whiteness of the blossoms rivalling the freshly fallen snow.

"Say, fellows, pinch me, will you?" Kenneth shouted down to his friends. "I've got a bad dream, I guess. All hands on deck to shovel snow." Kenneth's shout was very fierce. Frank appeared with a broom, Clyde with a dust pan, and Arthur brought a scrubbing brush.

"Pipe sweepers, mate," commanded the captain.

Arthur's whistle was a failure for the simple reason that one cannot pucker the mouth to whistle and laugh at the same time, but the crew understood, and all hands turned to and swept the decks free of snow.

"Pipe breakfast," was the next order. This was not necessary, however; all four boys tried to get through the two-foot-wide companionway at once, and all four stuck while the tantalizing odor of steaming coffee filled their nostrils. Clyde fell out of the bunch to the cabin floor, which relieved the jam and gave the others a chance.

At Vicksburg the boys tied up for four days and visited the bone of contention between the North and the South so many years ago. They found many reminders of the great siege— earthworks still plainly visible, the old stone house where Grant and Pemberton met to arrange for the surrender of the town.

Most impressive of all was the national cemetery—a great city of the dead. Then the boys realized as they never could by any other means the terrible struggle, the bravery shown on both sides, and the despair of the besieged as they were hemmed in more and more closely by the Union lines, while their ammunition gave out and food grew scarce. The travelers found that the war was still the chief topic of conversation in the south, and they got a point of view new to them. Events were still dated on the "time of the war," so it seemed as if the great conflict had taken place but a few years ago.

There was a new topic, however, that the northern boys could talk about without the least danger of giving offense. In the war with Spain, the sons of both Union and Confederate soldiers fought side by side, and the people on both sides of Mason and Dixon's line were equally proud of their achievements.

As the *Gazelle* got underway and sailed downstream, the boys looked back at the heights, while their thoughts carried them back to the time when Porter's fleets lay at anchor in about the same position and waited for the storm of iron from the guns mounted there to cease. But the wind was blowing half a gale, and their attention was called back with a jar from the past to the very practical present.

The stream was now very full and there was little danger of running aground, so Kenneth determined to sail in spite of the freshening wind and the steady drizzle that froze as it fell. It was Arthur's turn at the stick, but it was just the kind of weather to hurt one weakened by illness, so Kenneth took his place and sailed the boat. The wind a little abaft the beam (another of the best points of sailing, according to Ransom), the little boat sped on, racing, seemingly, with the billows the gale kicked up.

The other three boys stayed below in comfort while the captain, wrapped in a big ulster and crowned with a yellow sou'wester, held the tiller and looked the part of the weather-beaten mariner down to the ground.

The wind was steady and very strong, so that the yacht keeled over before it and almost buried her lee rail under; the sails rounded out to the blast, and as the rain froze on them, the rigging, the spars and the deck, she looked like a great candied boat, such as the confectioners like to display in their store windows. It was exhilarating, this flying along in the wintry air, but the frozen rigging and stiffened sheets made sailing difficult and dangerous. It would be impossible to reef and difficult to lower the canvas under these conditions.

With eyes alert and ready hand on tiller, Kenneth watched for snags, reefs or sandbars while cold rain dashed into his face in spite of the close-drawn sou'wester. Mile after mile the good craft sped on—swift, sure and steady. Past islands low-lying and gray in the mist, past forests of cypress, white and glistening with frost, the gray moss hanging from the branches, sleet covered and crackling in the wind. It was a run to remember, a run that stimulated, yet at the same time left the steersman surprisingly tired, as Ransom found when he tried to work his stiffened limbs and help furl the canvas.

"I wish that this sail had a few hinges," Frank complained, as he thumped it in a vain endeavor to roll it up compactly. "Might as well try to roll up a piece of plank."

It took over an hour to get things stowed properly that under ordinary circumstances could have been disposed of in 15 minutes; and though the captain firmly intended to write up his log that night, it was only by the exercise of a good deal of will power that he kept awake until supper was over.

The following day the *Gazelle* lay close to the levees of Natchez, having covered the distance of 93 miles in less than a day and a half.

This old town the boys thought the most beautiful that they

had seen. The stately old mansions were surrounded by gardens, and trees grew everywhere.

The town crowned the last of the heights of the Mississippi, and the view from the bluff is one of the finest anywhere along the river. Before starting on the cruise, the boys had read about the places they were likely to visit, and they recalled that Natchez was one of the earliest settlements on the river. They remembered, too, that the Natchez Indians, perhaps the most intelligent of their race, were one of the ten first tribes to run foul of the white man's civilization. Swift and sure pacification, by means of the sword, was their lot.

Natchez Under The Hill, as the cluster of houses occupying the narrow strip of land between the river and the steep slope is called, was an unattractive and foul as Natchez proper was beautiful and wholesome. Not many years ago it bore the reputation of being one of the hardest places on the Mississippi, and even when the boys anchored off its waterfront, they found it far from desirable.

A run of 139 miles in three days brought the *Gazelle* and her crew to Baton Rouge. Though the wind was blowing hard when they reached the town, they had to be content with the meager shelter of a few scattered trees on a low point. It was practically an open anchorage.

"Looks squally," Arthur remarked as he tied the last stop on the furled mainsail. "How's the glass?"

"Going down like thunder," Ransom answered from below. "Thermometer shows 15 degrees. Gee, I hope this wind lets up."

"Shall I put out the other anchor?" the mate inquired. It was a precaution Kenneth thought wise to take.

"I'll bet we have troubles to burn tonight," the skipper said half to himself as he lashed down everything movable with light line and rope yarn.

By the time supper was finished, the wind was howling through the rigging like a thousand demons. The little ship tugged at her anchors and bobbed up and down over seas that grew more turbulent each moment.

The usual cheerful talk, jests and snatches of songs were much subdued, or indeed, entirely lacking this night. Instead, the four sat and talked abstractedly with lowered voices and, from time to time, the talker would interrupt himself to listen to some peculiarly vicious blast.

The light of the pendent lamp, as it swung with the motion of the boat, cast strange, distorted, dancing shadows, and the boys sat close together as they listened to the howling of the wind. They were not afraid, but the agitation of the elements, the wind, the cold, and the continuous jumping and staggering motion of the yacht sent uncomfortable chills down their spines.

"I'll play you Pedro." Kenneth's voice sounded strangely loud in the cabin. He felt that it was not good to sit still and listen to the tempest.

The table was propped up and the cards dealt, but it was playing under difficulties—someone had to keep his hand on the cards played to make them stay on the table. They boys' hearts were not in it and they made absurd mistakes. Kenneth rallied them and tried in every way to steer their thoughts away from the danger, the tempest and the cold, but in spite of all he could do, the boys stopped playing and listened with all their ears. The hum of the rigging, the slap of the waves against the sides, the quick snap-snap of the tight drawn halyards against the masts—all contributed to the mighty chorus in honor of the gale.

Of a sudden there was a heavy thud and then a sliding sound, a sound different from all the other voices of the storm.

"What was that?" It was hard to tell whether it was one voice or four that uttered the words. The boys sprang to their feet and stood for a brief moment, listening.

AN ICY STORM OFF "SUNNY" BATON ROUGE

On the alert but motionless, the four boys waited for a repetition of the strange noise, wondering what it meant. The wind still shrieked; all the pandemonium of sound continued, but the queer sound was not repeated; neither was the unusual jar.

Kenneth was the first to move. He jumped to the companionway and pushed at the hinged doors leading on deck, but they did not move. Glued with the frost, they refused to open. He put his shoulder against them and pushed with all his might. The expected happened—the doors opened suddenly and Kenneth found himself sprawling on the floor of the cockpit. He skinned his shin on the brass-bound step of the companionway ladder and his funny bone tingled from a blow it got on the deck.

The boy tried to rise to his feet, but a sudden swing of the boat made him slip on the icy boards and fall swiftly down again. From his prone position, he looked around him. The light coming up through the open companionway gleamed yellow on the ice-coated, glistening boom, and the furled sail propped up in the crotch.

As Ransom's eyes became accustomed to the darkness, he saw what it was that had startled them all. *His Nibs*, hauled up on the narrow strip of deck aft of the rudder post had slipped when the *Gazelle* had made a sudden plunge and, sliding on the icy rail, had thumped into the cockpit. Perfectly safe, but ludicrously out of place, the little boat looked like a big St. Bernard in a lady's lap.

"Look!" the prostrate captain called to his friends. "*His Nibs* was getting lonesome and was coming down into the cabin for the sake of sociability."

The other three crawled on deck, having learned caution through the skipper's mishap, and crouched in the wet, slippery cockpit while they looked around.

The gale, still increasing rather than abating, was raising tremendous seas. The *Gazelle* rolled, her rails under at times, and her bowsprit jabbed the white-capped waves.

"I am going forward to see if the anchors are okay." Kenneth spoke loudly enough, but the wind snatched the words from his mouth and the boys did not hear what he said. Ransom managed to get on his feet and, grasping the beading of the cabin, he pulled himself erect. A quick lurch almost threw him overboard, but he reached up and grabbed the boom overhead just in time. Holding onto this with both arms, he slowly worked himself forward.

The other boys, crouching in the cockpit, wondered what he was up to. They watched his dim figure crawling painfully along, and once their hearts came into their throats as, his feet slipping from under him, he hung for an instant from the icy boom almost directly over the raging river. The light streaming from the cabin shone into their strained, anxious faces and blinded them so that they could hardly see the figure of Ken, on whom they had learned to rely. At last he disappeared altogether behind the mast and was swallowed up in the blackness.

"Ken! Come back! Come back!" Arthur, who was still weak, could not stand the strain; he could not bear to think of what might happen to his friend.

The wind shrieked in derision—so, at least, it seemed to the anxious boy. The elements combined to drown his voice. The gale howled on, the rain froze as it fell and the waves dashed at the boys like fierce dogs foaming at the mouth.

Frank, at last feeling that he must know what had become of Ransom, sprang up and, grasping the icy spar, crept forward. Many times he lost his foothold, but always managed somehow to catch himself in time. Slipping and sliding, fighting the gale, he reached the mast. The journey was one of only 20 feet, but the gale was so fierce and the exertion of keeping his footing so great that he arrived at the end out of breath and almost exhausted.

The night was inky black, and only with difficulty could he distinguish the familiar objects on the forecastle—the bitts and the two rigid anchor cables leading from it. Lying across them was Kenneth, gripping one, while the yacht's bow rose and fell, dashing the spray clear over his prostrate figure.

"What's the matter, Ken?" Frank shouted, so as to be heard above the wind. "Are you hurt? Brace up, old man!"

The other did not speak for a minute. Then he answered in a strained voice, "Give me a hand, old chap, will you? I've hurt my foot—wrenched it, I guess. Pains like blazes."

That he was pretty badly hurt, Frank guessed by the way in which he drew in his breath as he shifted his position. "Got a hold there, Frank? Grab those halyards. It's terribly slippery—Ouch! Easy, now."

It was a difficult job that Frank had in hand. The ice-covered decks could not be depended on at all. If the boys began to slide, they would slip right off the sloping cabin roof into the water. The boat was jumping on the choppy seas like a bucking horse, and the wind blew with hurricane force. Kenneth could help himself hardly at all, and Frank struggled with him until the sweat stood out on his brow in great beads. At last both got over the entangling anchor cables and, breathing hard, hugged the stick as if their lives depended on it, which came very near to being the case.

"You'd—better—leave me here—old chap," panted Kenneth. "My ankle—hurts like—the old—Harry. Can't—travel much."

"What did you do to it?

"Got caught—under cleat—on the butt—of the—bowsprit."

"Gee! That's tough!" sympathized Frank.

"Gave it a terrible wrench—regular monkey wrench." It was a grim situation to joke about.

"Leave you here?!" said Frank, coming back to Ken's suggestion. "I guess not! What do you take me for, anyway? I know how to work it all right. You hang on to the mast a minute."

Releasing his grip on Ransom, Chauvet picked up the end of the peak halyard coiled at his feet and, with great difficulty, straightened out its frozen turns, for he had but one free hand. He could not release his hold on the sailhoop that he grasped for an instant. Taking the stiff line, he passed it around his body and then around the boom. Holding on by his legs to the mast, he worked away at the frozen line until he had knotted the end to the main part—made a bowline. The loop was around his waist and the boom.

"Now, Ken, we're all right—I have lashed myself to this spar, and my hands are free. I'll yell to Clyde," and suiting the action to the word, he shouted aft.

Ransom hung on to the line about Frank's waist, while Frank half held, half supported him. Slowly they moved along, stumbling, often swinging with the boat, until the rope cut into Chauvet's body cruelly. It was exhausting work.

Soon Clyde came stumbling, slipping and fighting forward against the gale, and in a minute was helping Frank to support the gritty captain.

It was a thankful group that dropped into the warm, bright cabin, dripping wet and numbed with cold, out of breath, well-nigh exhausted, but thankful to the heart's core. Arthur cut the shoe from Ransom's swelling ankle and bound it tightly with a cloth saturated with witch hazel.

"Chasing anchors on stormy nights seems to be fatal for me," Kenneth remarked as he lay on his bunk regarding his bandaged foot. "I'll give you fellows a chance next time—I don't want to be piggish about it."

Presently the cabin light was turned down and all hands got into their berths. Not a tongue moved, but brains were active; not an eyelid felt heavy, but the boys resolutely kept them closed. The storm raged on; gust succeeded gust, and the rain beat down on the thin cabin roof with increasing fierceness. It was a trying night, and each of the four boys was glad enough to see the gray light come stealing in through the frosted port lights. They had all thought that they would never see daylight again, though each had kept his fears to himself.

The wind still roared and the rain poured down, but the yacht tossed and rolled less violently; her movements were slower and sluggish, quite unlike those of the usually sprightly, light *Gazelle*.

"Sea must have gone down," commented Clyde in a casual way as he noted that the others were awake. "Queer, wind's blowing great guns, too."

Kenneth sat up suddenly and bumped his head on the deck beam above. This made him wince and he drew his game foot suddenly against the boat's side. Kenneth made so wry a face that his friends could not help laughing outright—an honest laugh, in spite of the sympathy they felt.

"Both ends at once." The captain tried to rub his head and his ankle at the same moment and found it a good deal of a stretch.

"There is a new bar to be charted here." His finger went gingerly around the bump on his forehead. "Frank, go on deck, will you, and see if things are moderating. I'd like to get into some cove or another."

Chauvet made his way to the ladder and shoved the doors with all his might; but it was only after repeated blows with a heavy rope fender that they opened.

"Great Scott!" he shouted. "Look here. Ice! Why, there's no boat left—it's all ice! Well, I'll be switched—why, we'll have to chop her out, or she'll sink with the weight of it—she's down by the head now."

Fresh exclamations of amazement followed as each head appeared in turn from below. It was true. The yacht was literally covered with ice, from one to six inches thick at the bow, where the spray combined with the rain to add to the layers of white coating. The sluggish movement of the vessel was explained: the weight of the ice burdened her. Here was a pleasing condition of things.

The boys snatched a hasty breakfast and, taking hatchets, hammers—anything with a sharp edge—they attacked the ice. Even Ransom insisted upon taking a hand. The boat was very beautiful in her glassy coating. The rigging, fringed with icicles, and the cold, gray light shining on the polished surface made it look like a dull jewel. The boys, however, saw nothing of the beautiful side of it. There was a mighty job before them, a cold, hard, dangerous job, and they went at it as they had done with all the previous difficulties which they had encountered—with courage and energy.

Colder and colder it grew until the thermometer registered

five degrees below zero. The yacht still rolled and pitched so that the boys found it necessary to lash themselves to mast, spars and rigging while they chopped. The spray flew up and dashed into their faces and almost instantly froze. The sleeves of their coats became as hard and as stiff as iron pipes, and their hands stiffened so that the fingers could not hold the axe helves. Every few minutes one or the other would have to stop, go below and thaw out. They worked desperately, but new layers of frost formed almost as fast as the boys could hack it off. But chop and shovel they must or sink in plain sight of the town, as inaccessible as if the boat were miles from shore.

How they ever lived through the three days during which the storm continued, God, who saved them, alone knows. It seemed almost a miracle that so small a craft should have survived what it did.

When at the end of the weary time the wind subsided, the yacht rode over the choppy waves in much the same buoyant way as before—she was weatherproof—but her crew was utterly exhausted. Hands and faces were cut and bleeding from the fierce onslaught of the sleet-laden wind; fingers, toes and ears were frostbitten; innumerable bruises, true badges of honor, covered their bodies; and the captain suffered intolerably from his injured ankle.

"Hours chopping ice off the *Gazelle* to keep her from sinking under the weight of it," quoted Kenneth from the entry in his log, "and this in the heart of the 'Sunny South.'"

"I don't believe there is any 'Sunny South.'" Clyde was tired out and his sentiments expressed his condition.

"Remember the old fellow at Natchez?" said Frank. "He must have been a twin of Methuselah; he said he had never seen ice on the river so far south before, and he had lived on the Mississippi all his life."

It was many, many hours before the *Gazelle* was free enough of her burden to allow the crew to rest, and not until three days of gale had spent its spite upon them could she be got underway and anchored in a sheltered spot.

After sending reassuring letters to anxious ones at home, the *Gazelle* sped southward, seeking a sheltered spot to lie by and allow the ice which was sure to follow to pass by. At the little town of St. Gabriel's the *Gazelle* found a snug nest where, for a time, the ice ceased from troubling, and she floated secure.

It was with a grateful heart that Kenneth rose on Sunday morning, February 19th, and from the safe anchorage saw the great cakes of ice go racing by on the swift current.

"We can't hold a service aboard," he said to Arthur, who appeared on deck about the same time. "But let's dress ship for a thanksgiving offering."

All four agreed with alacrity and for the next hour scarcely a word was spoken except as one fellow sung out, "Where is that swab?" or another, "Who's got the bath-brick?"

Hardly a day passed (except when the boat was in actual danger) that the *Gazelle* did not get a thorough cleaning—brasses shined, decks scrubbed, cabin scoured, bedding aired, dishes well washed and even the dishcloth cleaned and spread to dry. But this was a special day, and the yacht was as sweet within as soap and water, elbow grease and determined wills could make her. The crowning of the work came when the *Gazelle* was decked in her colors, the flags spelling her name in the international code fluttering in the breeze, and above all Old Glory—surely a splendid emblem of what these youngsters gallantly typified, American perseverance, pluck and enterprise.

It was a proud crew that lined up on the bank to admire their achievement, and their hearts were filled with gratitude to Providence that they had been brought through so many dangers safely.

"Kin I hab one of dese yer flags?" Someone pulled at Kenneth's sleeve, and he looked down into the small, black, kinky-hair framed face of a little girl, scantily clad and shivering in the keen air.

"What do you want it for?"

Embarrassment showed on every shining feature of the little face.

"Fo'—fo' a crazy quilt," she managed to say at last.

Ransom could not spare one of his flags, but he dug into a locker and pulled out a piece of red flannel (a token of his mother's thoughtfulness) which pleased the little girl almost as much. The visits of the local population were frequent that day, and the many requests for "one of dose flags" suggested the thought that the first youngster had spread the news that the ship's company could be worked.

Two days later the ice had almost disappeared and the *Gazelle* left her snug berth for the last stretch of her journey to the Crescent City. The delay seemed to add to the yacht's eagerness to be gone, for she sped on her way like a horse on its first gallop after a winter in the stable. On and on she flew, drawing nearer to her goal, scarred from contact with ice, snags and sandbars, but still unhurt, triumphant. Surely the sun was rewarding their persistence, for he no longer hid his face from them but shone out in all mellowness and geniality. Their worries fled at his warm touch, and their hearts sang his praises.

The *Gazelle* seemed glad as she forged ahead, as if to say, "Hurrah! I have conquered. I have stood old Mississippi's bumps and jars! All these are of the past, and now for Old Ocean!"

Light after light was passed and marked off on the list, and soon the last one shone out. It had no name, so as they lustily gave three cheers for the last of the little beacons which had so long been their guides and dubbed it "Omega," the *Gazelle* sped on with only the smoke of the great cotton market as a guide. New Orleans was in sight.

The pillars of smoke—the smoke of the city of their dreams—led them on. They could hardly realize that the dim cloud, that dark streak in the distance, was really the city which they had striven so hard to reach.

A feeling of great satisfaction came over them as the *Gazelle* responded to the tiller, which was thrown hard down, and headed into the wind. A few flaps of the sails in the evening breeze, the sudden splash of the anchor forward, followed by the whir of the cable as it ran through the chocks, and the creaking pulleys as the sails were lowered, was the music in honor of the *Gazelle*'s successful voyage from faraway Michigan to New Orleans.

The trip of 1,800 miles had been full of incident and some satisfaction, purchased, however, at the price of severe toil and many hardships, with a decided preponderance of troubles over pleasures. Sickness had visited the crew at a time when their location made medical aid impossible. The most severe winter recorded, accompanied by the ice packs and low stages of water, made it seem many times as if all hands were indeed candidates for admission into the realms of Davy Jones's locker.

But all this was now of the past, for here was the *Gazelle* anchored in a snug cove in the outskirts of the southern metropolis, safe and sound, the captain and crew strong, well, happy, and in all ways improved by their struggles.

The sun was still two hours high when Kenneth and Frank rowed ashore in *His Nibs* and scrambled up the steep side of the high levee which protects the city from inundation.

As they looked back on the *Gazelle* so peacefully riding at her anchorage, they felt like giving three lusty cheers for their floating home. Beyond the yacht and moored at the docks were two immense ocean-going steamships, while a short distance up the river was a full-rigged ship with loosened canvas falling in graceful folds from the yards. The scene was a pleasing one, and the two boys drank it in with their eyes; they loved the sea, and these monster boats had a particular charm for them. But the "clang, clang" of a bell suddenly awakened them from their reverie, and they started in all haste to get downtown for the mail they knew must be waiting.

The anchorage was at Carrollton, one of the suburbs of New Orleans, so the boys had a splendid opportunity of seeing the city on their long trolley-car journey to the main post office. The batch of mail that was handed to them gladdened their hearts, and it took considerable resolution to refrain from camping out on the post office steps and reading their letters. They remembered, however, their promise to Arthur and Clyde to bring back with them the wherewithal to make a feast in honor of their safe arrival in the Crescent City.

"Gee! I'd like to know what's in those letters." Frank gazed at them longingly as they walked along. "Look at the fatness of that, will you?"

"I've got a fat one, myself," retorted Kenneth, holding a thick letter bearing several stamps. "We have just about time enough to buy some truck and get back. What do you say to some oysters?"

"That goes," was Frank's hearty endorsement.

Oysters were cheap, they found, so they bought a goodly

supply and, for want of a better carrier, put them in a stout paper bag.

The two boys started out bravely with the bag of oysters between them, each carrying a bundle of papers and mail under their arms. They saw many things that interested them—quaint, old buildings with balconies and twisted ironwork, and numbers of picturesque, dark-skinned people wearing bright colors wherever it was possible.

Frank and Kenneth were so interested in watching what was going on about them—the people, the buildings, and all the hundred and one things that would interest a northern boy in a southern city—that they forgot all about the load of oysters until they noticed that the people who met and passed them were smiling broadly.

"Have I got a smudge on my nose, Frank?" asked Kenneth, trying vainly to squint down that member.

"No, have I?" Frank's answer and question came in the same breath.

"Well, what in thunder are these people grin——?"

There was a soft, tearing sound, and then a hollow rattle. The boys looked down quickly and saw that the damp oysters had softened the paper so that the bag no longer held them, and they were falling, leaving a generous trail behind them.

Frank and Kenneth scratched their heads; there were no shops near at hand, the bag was no earthly use, they were a long way from the anchorage, and the oysters were much too precious to be abandoned.

"What's the matter with tying up the sleeves of this old coat and making a bag of it?" Fran's inventive brain was beginning to work.

"That's all right, if you don't object," was the reply.

An hour later two boys, one of them in his shirt sleeves, came stumbling along in the dusk toward the levee near which the *Gazelle* was anchored.

"*Gazelle*, ahoy! they hailed. "Have you got room for a bunch of oysters and a couple of appetites?"

Evidently there was plenty of room, for *His Nibs* came rushing across to take all three, the bunch of oysters and the two appetites, over to the yacht, where they found two more appetites eagerly waiting their coming.

Ransom and his friends had planned to stay but ten days in New Orleans, just time enough to put in a new mast and refit generally for the long sea voyage before them. Their good intentions, however, were balked at every turn. The parents of all the boys, except Ransom's, besought them to return, making all sorts of inducements to persuade them to give up the trip, and doing everything in fact, except actually command them. A death in Clyde's family made it imperative that he should go back, and it grieved the boys to have him leave. Clyde was as disappointed as any, and as he boarded the train to go north, he said, "I'd give a farm to be coming instead of going."

The crew was now reduced to three, and Ransom feared that Clyde's return would influence the others and break up the cruise. The letters to Frank and Arthur grew more and more insistent until one day Chauvet came to Ransom. "Ken," he said, "this is getting pretty serious. My people come as near saying that they'll disown me if I don't come back as they can without actually writing the words. I want to go the rest of the way and play the whole game, and it would be a lowdown trick to leave you stranded here without a crew."

"Well," said Kenneth, as he sat down by Frank's side on the levee in the warm sunshine, "you'll have to do as you think best, but—I never told you that my father and mother offered me their house if I would give up the trip, did I?"

Frank opened his eyes at this.

"No, I didn't, but it's a fact; and when I told them that I didn't have to be paid to stay and would not go if they felt so strongly about it, they came right around and said, 'Go, and God bless you.'"

Kenneth's eyes moistened a little as he harked back to the time, and a vivid picture of his faraway northern home arose before him. "Well, old chap," he continued, laying his hand on Frank's knee, "they have been with me heartily ever since, and I believe that your people would feel the same about you and be proud of your pluck, too."

The two looked each other in the eyes a minute—one fair, the other dark, utterly dissimilar in appearance, but both possessed of indomitable will and courage. Then Frank's hand slowly sought that of his friend and gripped it hard.

"Ken, I'm with you."

"Good," was the other's only answer.

Arthur's decision was soon made when he found that Kenneth and Frank had determined to put it through. The three were knit together in a bond of fellowship hard to break.

The equinoctial storms were raging through the Gulf at this period, and the boys made good use of the time to buy, shape and put in place a new main mast, to tighten up the rigging, and to repaint the boat's sides, covering up the scars left by the inhospitable river. *His Nibs* was also refitted, so that the staunch little craft looked like new and was much admired.

The boys rambled all over the old city, from the above-ground, tomb-like cemetery to the lively Creole quarter. Ransom visited many ships in port and studied the lines and construction of ocean-going vessels, river craft and lugger fishing boats. All sorts of craft congregated at this harbor for all kinds of purposes: for cotton, for sugar, for every sort of commodity, in fact, even down to mules. Ransom watched them all, went aboard some and talked with the mates and engineers. His intelligent questions won him courteous, thoughtful answers. He took notes, made sketches, and in every way possible took advantage of this opportunity to fit himself for his life's work.

At last, on the first of May, 1899, the storms having passed and the *Gazelle* being as fit and trim as a boat could be, the crew bade goodbye to the many friends they had made, cast off from their moorings and started for the salt sea.

For two days they sailed through the delta of the Mississippi before entering that dangerous short cut to the Gulf, Cubit's Gap, a passage flanked on either side by shoals which even the *Gazelle* could not sail over. It was lined with the skeletons of wrecked vessels, and made the boys hesitate a little before taking the risk. But "nothing ventured, nothing gained," they thought, and a successful venture would mean almost a hundred miles gained.

The weather conditions were good and the vote was unanimous in favor of trying so, on reaching the cut, the *Gazelle* turned to port and entered the dangerous channel.

"Goodbye, old Mississippi," Kenneth said, half aloud. "We are ocean-bound at last."

It was all done very quickly, and never a feeling of reluctance came over them as they carefully picked their way among the shoals of the pass.

The run through the sand point, which the current of the river had forced out into the Gulf, was some six miles long. By careful sailing the *Gazelle* ran this distance without mishap and then, spread out before her, was the great Gulf of Mexico. Ahead for several miles was the shallow shoal. Debris of every kind surrounded them. Everything was so lonesome, not a sail in sight or anything to make them feel that the world was peopled.

A flock of sea birds rose from the water and, with a peculiar cry, flew far away, as if frightened by a sight seldom seen. For a moment it seemed as if they were "alone on a wide, wide sea."

The sea was calm so, taking a sounding pole aboard *His Nibs*, Frank, with chart before him, measured the depth. The *Gazelle*, under shortened sail, followed slowly in his wake, often luffing quickly to avoid a bar and slowly but surely winding her way. So intricate did the path become at times that it was necessary for them to cast anchor and explore ahead for depths sufficient to float the yacht.

At last, just as the sun was sinking in the distant west, their labors were rewarded by success, for careful sailing and constant sounding were necessary, but at last the cheery cry of "No bottom!" came from their pilot ahead, and in a few minutes the staunch *Gazelle* was gliding along on the long, rolling surface of the open Gulf, afloat at last on the great salt sea.

ON SALTWATER AT LAST

"Hurrah for the sea, the blue salt sea, the sea that we strove to reach!" shouted Kenneth at the top of his voice.

"Hurrah!" shouted the other two boys, and all three clasped hands and danced about in glee.

"Isn't this worth working for?" inquired the captain, as he swept his hand around, tracing the horizon line.

Off in the distance lay the Bird Islands, and still further the Breton Islands showed faint and hazy in the fast-deepening dusk. The wind was a mere caressing zephyr, and the sea rolled in good-naturedly, soothingly, even.

"What's the matter with this, boys? Let's anchor here. Heave the lead, Frank, and see if it's all right."

Frank reached under the cockpit seat and took from its rack the lead and line. "Aye, aye, sir," he answered in mock servility. Hooking his left arm around the port stays, he stood on the rail, the long strip of lead dangling from his right hand, the coil of line in his left.

For a minute he stood poised there while the *Gazelle* curtseyed her acknowledgments to the long swells, a picturesque figure silhouetted against the warm glow of the setting sun. Then he began to swing his right arm slowly and steadily, the lead just clearing the water. When it was swinging well forward he let it go, and as the line slipped through his fingers he watched for the bits of colored cloth that indicated the depth. Down, down it went, until all but the leather strips had disappeared into the water. Then the line slackened and the leadsman knew that bottom had been reached. Beginning to pull in the line, Frank shouted, "Three fathoms!"

"Stand by! Let go your anchor!" ordered Kenneth as soon as Frank had reeled in the leadline.

"Let her go!"

There was a splash, then a hum and swish of heavy rope as the anchor cable whipped through the chocks.

"Let go your mizzen halyards!" The creak of the blocks told that the order had been obeyed. Arthur let the jigger go at the same time. For a few minutes not a word was spoken—all the mouths were full of cotton rope—"stops"—while the hands were busy tightly rolling the sails. The jib was furled up at last, and not until the anchor light was set glowing, hung from the triced-up jib four or five feet above the deck, did the four boys have time to lay off and enjoy the situation.

They were surprised to see how dark it was. Only a minute ago it seemed the sky was alight and full of color. Now only a faint, soft glow remained as a reminder that they were near the tropics, where the sun drops out of sight while still glowing.

Arthur and Kenneth lay on their backs on the cabin roof while Frank went below to get supper. Both boys murmured their content. They were a little tired, for the navigation of Cubit's Gap had been a strain on their nerves and had necessitated more or less violent exertion.

The air was warm and restful; the motion of the boat was like the easy rocking of a cradle, the most delightful motion on earth. The stars were just beginning to show themselves and the mast of the boat seemed to point them out one by one as she swung to and fro. Suddenly there was a slight splash alongside and a long-drawn, vociferous sigh.

"What was that?" Arthur said, sitting up quickly with a startled look on his face.

"I don't know," Ransom confessed, rubbing his eyes. "Queer, wasn't it?"

Frank's clatter as he made ready the supper were the only

sounds that could be heard

"Listen!"

Again the long sigh. It seemed to come from the very heart of someone in intense pain.

Both boys jumped up, and Arthur called softly to Frank to come on deck. Then all three leaned over the side, looking eagerly for the soul in torment. They half expected to see a white, upturned face showing against the dark water. Again the sound of escaping breath. The boys looked in the direction from whence it came and saw, not the white face of a drowning woman, nor anything else of a like nature, but the black, glistening hide of a huge porpoise as it leisurely humped its back and disappeared below the surface.

"Phew! but that scared me," remarked Arthur. "Thought somebody was in trouble, sure."

"The laugh is on us, all right," Kenneth said, but he shivered slightly in remembrance of the strange sound. "How's supper, Frank? I'm hungry enough to eat half that porpoise!"

It was a merry party that sat down to the meal of oysters, which had been given to them by their fisherman friends; spuds, as the boys called the potatoes; coffee, bread without butter, and a treasured pie, rather the worse for wear, but keenly relished for all that. What was left of the meal would not have satisfied a bird, and the dishwashing that night was an easy job.

All three of the boys felt that their fun was really only just beginning. The cruise down the Mississippi seemed like a nightmare as they looked back upon it. Cold, unending exertion, sickness and imminent danger, coupled with a necessity for great economy, had taken all the zest out of the enjoyment they might have had.

Something has been said about Ransom's financial condition; the same thing was true of the other boys. Clyde and Arthur hoped and expected to make some money along the way to help pay expenses, as did Kenneth and Frank, but fortune was against them and they had to get along as best they could on the small sums they possessed. From St. Louis to New Orleans, taking in all expenses, including extra oil needed to keep from freezing, medicines and extra nourishing food for the invalid Arthur, the total cost per boy per week was a dollar and a half.

It was no wonder, then, that all three thought a happier time was coming. Smiling, sunny skies above them and clear, buoyant saltwater under them, a tried and true ship their home and a ship's company that could absolutely be relied upon—what more was to be desired?

The night was divided into three watches of four hours each, and Kenneth went on deck to take the first trick from eight to twelve. So the young fresh-water sailors passed the first night on the briny deep. A peaceful, restful, invigorating night that marked the beginning of a new series of experiences.

Arthur went on at midnight (eight bells) and Frank, in turn, relieved Arthur at four o'clock (eight bells of the morning watch). It was Frank, then, who put his head into the after hatch and roused all hands at six o'clock, which Arthur and Kenneth called an unholy hour.

"I wonder if there are any sharks around," said Arthur as he stood on the dew-wet deck looking overboard. "Gee, that water looks tempting. Here goes!" Almost with a single sweep of his hands he had pulled off his duck jumper and trousers, and the last words ended in a gurgle as he hit the water.

"Beat you in," was Frank's only comment to Kenneth, who came on deck that minute. It was a dead heat. As for sharks, the thought of them did not enter the heads of the three boys as they ducked and dove, splashed and swam, shouted and squealed with pure delight. It would have upset the equilibrium of any self-respecting shark; at any rate, none made their appearance that day.

It was a very airy costume that the crew wore that morning while they scrubbed down decks, coiled down tackle, cleaned out *His Nibs* and put the little ship to rights generally.

Kenneth and Arthur got the *Gazelle* underway, while Frank went below to get breakfast. The course was shaped for Biloxi, Mississippi, and the yacht settled down to the two-day run. The wind was fair and true, and the yacht, spreading out her wings, sped between the many islands that dotted the waters, and picked her way through the intricate channels daintily.

They anchored off Barrell Key that night and made the acquaintance of two Austrian fishermen whose lugger was anchored close by. The boys accepted their invitation to fish with them the next morning, and while they did little more than contribute considerable looking on, they got a good mess of fish. These Frank speedily turned into an appetizing breakfast, the incense from which was still rising when the boys bid their fishermen friends goodbye. In a very short time the mast of the lugger had dwindled to a matchstick and the swift, rakish little hull disappeared below the horizon.

It was just dark enough to make it difficult to distinguish the channel marks when they reached Biloxi Harbor, but the mudhook was dropped in a safe place, and Frank and Kenneth went ashore to look for mail and to telegraph home the news of their safe arrival. They had been unable to send word for the better part of a week and the loss last year about the same time of a large launch, the *Paul Jones*, in the waters through which the *Gazelle* had navigated so serenely would, the boys knew, make their parents dread this part of the cruise. It was partly a feeling of triumph, partly a desire to relieve anxiety that Kenneth experienced as he hurried to wire home.

The teredo, that terrible little insect that turns the bottoms of vessels into sieves and undermines the woodwork of wharfs in southern waters, was very much on the mind (metaphorically, of course) of the young captain. He had no desire to feed the staunch *Gazelle* to the voracious little borer. Many times he had been warned to copper-paint the bottom of the yacht and, though he dreaded the job, the sooner it was done the better.

A sloping sand beach lay to one side of Biloxi, and onto this the *Gazelle* was hauled at high tide, her ballast unloaded, and as the water fell she careened to one side. The starboard side was exposed first and, to the delight and satisfaction of Kenneth and his friends, there was hardly a scratch in the clear, hard wood. All hands immediately fell to work scraping off the marine growth that had formed. It was a three-hour job, but when it was finished the boys felt so virtuous that satisfaction stuck out like the paint on their faces. "Pride goeth before a fall," but the oyster shell cut which Kenneth's foot received seemed to him a fall entirely out of proportion to the pride.

Invincible to the terrible teredo, the *Gazelle* sailed out of Biloxi

Harbor, bound for Mobile. She reached her destination the same day, just as the sunset gun of Fort Morgan boomed out and the Stars and Stripes came fluttering down its staff.

The *Gazelle*'s ensign came down at the same instant. "You see, we are recognized," Kenneth remarked airily, as he waved his hand in the direction of the cloud of gunpowder smoke that still hovered over the muzzle of the old smooth-bore.

There was some discussion as to who should go ashore and inspect the fort—the grassy slope that led up to the massive red-gray pile was very inviting—but eventually the strands of rope yarn decided for them that Kenneth should not go. Whereupon he declared that he ought not to walk on his injured foot, anyway.

After rowing in close to the grassy ramparts of the fortress, Frank and Arthur decided that they did not care to visit it, either. Whether Uncle Sam's soldier, who paced along close to the water and carried a gun, had anything to do with their sudden change of plan, is not for the writer to say, but Ransom noticed that the two would-be visitors seemed disinclined to talk about the matter.

The fishing was so good in Mobile Bay that the boys could literally stand at their hearthstone (if a boat can be said to have a hearthstone—galley hatch would be more correct), and catch their breakfast. If they could have been satisfied to live on fish alone, life would have been too easy.

"We will grow scales if we eat much more fish," said Kenneth the last day of their stay in Mobile Bay.

"That's a good scheme," enthused Arthur (he of the fertile imagination). "Then we could make no end of money exhibiting ourselves as the only original mermen."

Notwithstanding the possibilities of this enterprise, the three boys laid in a goodly supply of plain shore bread, potatoes, even a pickle or two, and filled the water breakers with fresh water; it would be two days before the next town could be reached.

Bright and early, Arthur, who had the morning watch, called all hands, and weighing anchor the *Gazelle*'s bowsprit was turned seaward. The long sandbar leading out from Mobile harbor was marked at its outer end by a whistling buoy that sped the parting guest most mournfully and welcomed the coming one with a dirge. The wave-driven billows produced a most melancholy whistle, and the boys were glad when they had turned to port and were beyond the sound of it.

Fickle fortune smiled on these hard-used voyagers at last. Blue skies overhead, the clear waters below, a delicate light green that reflected into the white sails, or a deep verdant color that was restful to the eye and showed off to advantage the tints of the jewel-like fish that swam in its depths. The warm sun—too warm at times—was a joy after the long, sunless days on the Mississippi, though it tanned their skins the color of the cherry-finished cabin.

Two days out from Mobile they were sailing along in a light breeze, almost dead aft. Frank held the tiller and was having little to do; Kenneth lay on his stomach in the cockpit, studying the chart with its multiplicity of figures showing depths of water; Arthur was below putting a very conspicuous background into a pair of his duck trousers.

"How's the weather up there, old man?" Arthur shouted to Frank.

"All right, all right!" came the answer drowsily. "Not much wind, but hotter than blazes."

"There's going to be trouble all the same, 'glass' shows it."

Kenneth came tumbling down to see and, sure enough, the barometer was falling fast. It did not seem possible that a storm could be coming. The air was bright and clear, the long easy swells suggesting nothing but good treatment, and the breeze was almost caressing in its softness. It was the calm before the storm.

Presently the warmth began to go out of the air, and a chilliness that made the boys shiver crept into it. A darkening came up in the southwest, which gradually deepened and spread until the whole heavens were deep blue-black, against which the scudding clouds showed white and ominous. From time to time the boys heard a distant rumbling, and streaks of zigzag lightning flashed across the gloom. It was the first time the *Gazelle* and her crew had encountered a blow on the salt water, and they looked to the shore for a shelter.

Vicious little blasts, advance pickets of the squall, blew sharply across the sea and picked up little puffs of spray which instantly disappeared in vapor. The *Gazelle* trembled under these slaps of wind like a spirited horse under the touch of a nervous driver.

The shore was without a vestige of shelter, and there was nothing to do but to ride it out.

Kenneth took the tiller while Arthur and Frank made haste to reef down. The mainsail was lowered altogether and furled, the jib was reefed twice and the jigger hauled inboard and reefed also. *His Nibs* was hauled aboard and lashed down tight. Oilskin coats and sou'westers were broken out of the lockers and the hatches were shut tight and battened down. The boat would have to do the rest to bring them through safely, and all had confidence that she would be perfectly able to do so.

These preparations were made none too soon. In an instant the sharp, little puffs of wind gave way to a whooping gale that picked up the sea and the yacht alike, and swept them like chaff before it along shore. Then came the rain—a deluge, a cataract, that shut down on everything like night. The sea rose up about them like moving hills, the wind buffeted them so that the yacht jarred with the blows, and the rain closed in on them, a watery stockade. It drenched the crew crouched in the cockpit through and through, and dashed into their faces a thousand stinging darts.

The squall lasted for an hour without letup. The *Gazelle* rode the waves beautifully and took the buffets of wind and rain like the sturdy craft she was, without a murmur. The sharp flashes of lightning gave Kenneth momentary glimpses of the shore by which he managed to steer. Otherwise they were going it blind.

At length they noticed that the volleys of thunder seemed less near, the lighting less frequent and the onslaught of the rain darts not so sharp. The squall began to die down as quickly as it rose. Astern a faint light showed, while ahead the gloom was as deep as before. The rain grew less and less, and then passed entirely; the sun cleared his brow and shone down amiably through a blue sky, the wind calmed to a steady breeze, rain-washed and cool. Only the troubled sea remained as a reminder of the tempest.

Frank got up and shook himself. "I wish we had a wringer aboard," he said. "I'd like to put myself through it. Ugh! I'm wet."

As the sun dropped into the sea, the *Gazelle* ran over the bar and anchored just inside of Pensacola Harbor. The ebb tide prevented them from going up to the town.

The shelter was slight and the sharp squall of the afternoon raised the sea to an uncomfortable degree of motion. The *Gazelle* tossed and rolled, not having the steadying advantage of spread canvas. The boys were glad enough when the sun rose and the tide allowed them to sail up to a sheltered anchorage off the city itself.

The thing about the city of Pensacola that seemed principally to attract the boys' interest was a large ice-manufacturing plant, the manager of which presented them with a sizable cake. This, to boys who had been drinking lukewarm, rather brackish water, was a real boon.

After leaving Pensacola Harbor they turned to port, and found anchored just around the bar a fleet of vessels flying the yellow quarantine flag. But the *Gazelle*, having a clean bill of health, gave them a wide berth and sped on.

The rather intricate passage into Santa Rosa Sound was run without mishap, and then began one of the most delightful day's sail of the cruise.

They passed a strip of sand hills 20 miles long, for the most part covered with tall, waving grass, live oaks and palms, but showing glimpses here and there of the white, gleaming sand. The mainland along the Sound is a government reservation, thickly planted with live oaks forming a solid wall of green almost 20 miles long—a hedge, as it were, with irregular top, showing where some ambitious tree has grown above its fellows. Between is a strip of water five miles wide, smooth and clear, light green in its shallows, shading into the deep blue that marked the channel.

Along this path of beauty flew the *Gazelle*, her white sides and sails gleaming against the tinted water.

A fleet of fishing boats was sailing ahead when the *Gazelle* entered the Sound, their graceful shapes skimming over the water.

Kenneth stood up in his place at the helm and looked at them. "The *Gazelle* has proved herself seaworthy," he said, rather proudly. "I bet she can beat that bunch of boats ahead."

There were no takers, but all hands watched the gap of water between the yacht and hindmost craft eagerly. The wind was astern and, with her sheets well out, the yawl flew after the fishing fleet. For an hour there was little change in the relative positions of the pursuer and the pursued; then the boys noticed that the distance was lessening. On they flew up the broad, ribbon-like channel, until they were almost able to read the names on the sterns of the working boats.

"We're not so slow," Kenneth cried as the *Gazelle* drew alongside, his eyes shining with pleasure.

"Adios," shouted a swarthy man standing in the stern sheets of a lugger. "Fine boat, yours; you want swap?" A set of white teeth shone as he smiled sunnily.

The three boys took off their caps and waved a salute. "No, thank you; we're bound up the Atlantic coast, need deep draft boat," Kenneth answered.

"Atlantic, that boat? No!" the other said, half to himself; and the last the boys saw of him he was still shaking his head emphatically.

"Doesn't know the boat, does he, boys?" Kenneth laughed.

The fishing fleet was soon left behind and the *Gazelle* was once more sailing alone. The sun began to sink lower and lower, gaining depth of color as it dropped, until the whole narrow path of water blazed and sparkled with opalescent tints. The boys were almost intoxicated with the delight of it, and did not notice how abruptly the sound was narrowing down. The sunset's glory was short-lived, however, and the crew found themselves in an intricate, crooked channel, utterly strange to them. They had almost decided to anchor when they noticed a large schooner, a mere shadow, gliding ahead of them.

"We'll follow her wake," declared Kenneth. "She knows the channel if we don't."

Like hounds on the trail they followed the schooner through the deepening dusk until the flapping of canvas told them that she had come into the wind and the clank of chain cable through the hawse pipes betrayed the fact that she had anchored.

Bright and early the next morning the rollicking three were overboard taking an awakening bath. After bidding goodbye to their guides of the night before, they began to pick their way among the bars and coral rocks to the open Gulf. It was trying, careful work, requiring constant watchfulness, frequent sounding and much tacking to and fro; but the *Gazelle* was riding the long swells of the open sea by eight o'clock. A long sail was ahead of them and they hoped to make the distance to St. Joseph's Bay by nightfall, a run of about 80 miles.

But alas! The wind forsook them, and hour after hour they rolled on the long, oily swells under the brazen sun.

"I am tired of loafing around. I am going to do something." Arthur got up from his place on the deck aft and looked around for a suggestion.

Frank and Kenneth started at this sudden display of energy.

"What are you going to do?" Kenneth asked.

"Fish," was Arthur's laconic answer as he caught sight of a stout line with a big hook bent on it.

"Going to catch minnows?" Frank suggested facetiously.

"No, whales."

Arthur went below and dug out of the locker the end of a piece of pork. Then, dropping the tackle and bait into *His Nibs*, he pushed off.

Kenneth roused himself. "Say, Arthur," he called, "better fish from the yacht; we might catch a breeze and leave you."

"Oh, go away," the mate answered. "There isn't a breeze within 200 miles of here."

Arthur rowed off a hundred yards or so, baited his hook and dropped it overboard.

"Well, if he isn't the greatest freak," Frank remarked lazily.

For some time the two boys on the yacht watched him; then, as nothing happened, they moved their gaze, half dozing in the warm, salt air.

Of a sudden there was a cry and a thump as of wood against wood. They looked quickly and saw Arthur hanging on to the line which stretched out before him tight as a harp string. The boat was rocking dangerously and the oars banged together.

"What's the matter?" both boys shouted.

"I have caught something," was the answer.

He certainly had caught something; and the "something" was carrying him rapidly away from the *Gazelle* out to sea.

RIDING A MONSTER TURTLE

After rowing away from the yacht, Arthur dropped his baited hook overboard and, for a time, waited eagerly for something to happen. But the water remained as before, the sun shone down with unabated ardor and the heat waves danced over the shining sea. He soon lost interest and sat drowsily, holding the line loosely in his hand, his white canvas hat drawn over his eyes.

Suddenly there was a jerk, and the line began to burn through his fingers. He gripped it hard and was nearly pulled overboard. The thing at the other end, surprised at resistance, stopped an instant and gave Arthur time to recover himself.

"Gee, I've got something!" he shouted. He certainly had, or something had got him. It was some time before he could make up his mind which it was.

The fish began to move. Arthur determined he should not, and the consequence was that they all moved—the fish, *His Nibs* and Arthur—straight for the open Gulf.

"Here, where are you going?" Kenneth's voice came faintly over the water to him.

"I don't know," Arthur shouted back, his eyes on the taut line.

"Cut loose!" The voice from the yacht was fainter. Arthur thought that he must be moving away fast, but he determined that he would not give up. He watched the line closely, and presently noticed that it was taking a longer and longer slant; evidently the fish was coming to the surface. *His Nibs* rushed along at a great rate, its bow low down with Arthur's weight and the stress of the towing, its stern almost out of the water. The line rose slowly until it was almost parallel with the surface. Arthur watched it excitedly as it cut the water like a knife and the drops were thrown aside by its vibrations. At length a sharp fin rose out of the water and cut a rippling V in the blue sea.

"By Jove! It's a shark!" said Arthur between his teeth.

The boys on the yacht evidently saw, too, for a faint cry reached the ears of the boy in the boat. "Let him go!" they shouted. "Let him go!"

"I'll be hanged if I do." Arthur did not waste his breath by speaking the words aloud; he needed all his strength to hold on to the small line. The cord cut his fingers and the pull made his arms ache, but he would not give in. "That beast must get tired sometime," he thought. Suddenly the fin turned, there was a miniature whirlpool behind it, and Arthur's arms were nearly wrenched out as the shark put help to port and struck out in a new direction. Arthur looked up, saw that they were heading straight for the *Gazelle* and took courage.

"If only he'll go near enough," thought the boy; but the capture was not to be counted on, as it dashed from side to side and made rushes this way and that in a vain endeavor to get away from the maddening hook. Its general direction, however, was toward the yacht. Arthur shouted: "Soak him if you get a chance. I'm nearly done."

In one of its mad rushes the shark came within ten yards of the yacht when Frank, making a lucky cast with the heavy sounding lead, landed it on the beast's most vulnerable spot, the nose, and stunned him. Arthur got out an oar and paddled over to the yawl, handed the line over to Frank and got aboard. Frank made the line fast to the bitts forward, then cried exultantly: "Go ahead, old tow-horse, and tow away. Pleased to have you, I'm sure." The shark's gameness was broken, however, and after a few heroic struggles to get free it came within easy sight of Frank, who speedily put a bullet into him and ended the tragedy. They pulled the great fish alongside and measured him.

"A good twelve-footer, I bet," Frank asserted, after measuring the big tiger of the sea with an oar. "And look at that jaw! Jonah could only have got past those teeth in sections."

"Well, you did do something," Kenneth remarked as he glanced at the long, lithe creature floating alongside. "But I did not expect you to catch a towboat."

"Suppose—say, I've got a bright idea." Frank looked up from his inspection of Arthur's catch. "Suppose we drop a couple of baited lines forward, made fast to the bitts, catch a team of sharks and get towed to our next port, or why not the whole distance?"

"It might be all right to start, but how the mischief would we stop?" Arthur rubbed his muscles, strained in the efforts which he had already made in that direction.

"Oh, just anchor, hobble our team by the tails and go on about our business. It's as simple as can be. They could soon be taught port and starboard."

"Coming down to plain facts, I wish we had a breeze; even a foot-pump would help us." Kenneth shielded his eyes from the glare and looked over the glittering blue waters for a wind ripple.

"Yes, like that fellow back in Michigan who proposed to put a motor in his boat with an air blower, so that when the wind gave out he could blow himself along."

Only enough breeze ruffled the smooth waters of the Gulf to allow them to creep back into harbor and wait for a new day. The shark was cast loose, in spite of Arthur's impractical protest that he wanted to keep it as a souvenir.

The next morning all hands were up early and greeted as they came on deck by a spanking southwest wind. It was more than a breeze; it might be ranked as a reefing wind, but the *Gazelle* was under-canvassed and so hoisted full sail safely. The whole aspect of the sea had changed. Deep, blue and rippling under the steady wind, it had lost the brazen glare of the day before. The palms along shore waved their graceful fronds in gentle salutation, and the white-crested breakers made obeisance at their feet.

"Up anchor and away, boys!" Kenneth shouted, exhilarated by the ozone in the air. Frank and Arthur started to work the small hand windlass. "Put your backs to it, boys; we'll be off the sooner."

In a minute the anchor broke ground; the yacht began to pay off and was underway in earnest.

"Gee! This is better than your old shark-towing scheme," Arthur said, as he and Frank coiled down the gear and made all snug for the long day's run. "There's nothing like a windjammer, say I."

"Right you are, Art," Frank acknowledged. "My! I am hungry, though; my breastbone is flat against my spine."

"Well, it's up to you, old man," Kenneth sang out from his place in the cockpit. "Chase it along; I feel as if I could eat Arthur's shark."

As the day wore on, the waves grew larger, long rounded rollers that at times crested and were blown into spray by the wind. Huge, tumbling, rolling hills they were, like great play fellows, mighty but amiable. The boys felt a kind of fellowship for them and enjoyed watching the blue-green slopes that rose and fell, now hiding the land from them, now lifting boat and all to a watery height, widening the horizon and giving the boys little thrills of delight as they coasted down into the hollows again.

Hour after hour they sailed on, the wind steady and true from the southwest so that only the slightest shift of the helm was necessary and tending sheet became a sinecure. The *Gazelle* even acted as if she were enjoying herself. She ran up the hill of one wave and down the slope of another, like a frolicsome dolphin with a superabundance of animal spirits. Indeed, the porpoises seemed to recognize in her a playfellow, for they somersaulted along in company with her for hours, mocked at her grace, raced with her and dove under her, for all the world like children at play.

"Jiminy! Let's have a swim with 'em," said Arthur, who, fascinated by their easy antics, was positively envious. "If I could swim like that, I wouldn't mind turning my feet into fins one bit."

The delights of that day's sail would fill a book. The strange fish which they caught glimpses of as the yawl flew along, brilliantly colored and flashing like jewels in the clear depths; schools of flying fish, strange, specter-like creatures, sprang out of the blue and scudded a hundred feet or so clear of the waves, then dropped as suddenly as they had risen into their native element again.

Still the good yacht sped on swiftly, steadily, like a great, tireless bird. To starboard the boys could see nothing but the same old sea, the same, but always changing, always new. To port, the land was fringed with white tossing breakers, and beyond that forests of trees, graceful palms and sturdy live oaks with their branches draped in swaying moss, made a background of exquisite beauty. Here and there a veritable giant that had lost in its battle with the elements rose up above the rest, bare, denuded and black, but a sturdy relic still.

After a four-hour trick at the stick, Kenneth gave up the helm to Arthur and went below to write up his log. For a time the other two boys could see him laboring with a pen at the big, ledger-like book, intent on doing what he considered his duty, but his hand traveled slowly, then more slowly still. He looked up to get ideas, glanced through the oval port lights, now shut in by a green wall of sunlit water or giving a sudden glimpse of blue, cloud-flecked sky and palm-clad land over the heaving waters. For a time he gazed, then, frowning, grasped his pen determinedly and set to work again. A dozen lines, perhaps, were written; then his eyes were irresistibly drawn again to the ever-changing pictures of sea and sky in the oval frames.

"Better give it up, old man," Frank shouted down the hatch, laughing. "Save your log 'til you can't do anything else, or until it's too dark to see. This is better than a hundred logs. Come on deck and see it all. You can tell about it later."

"I can't resist; that's a fact," Kenneth answered, coming on deck. "This beats anything I ever even heard of. Don't the old boat sail through, though? Steady as a church—skates up and down the waves as if she enjoyed it."

The boys went below only to eat. Frank and Kenneth washed dishes because Arthur was sailing. This was according to the unwritten law that the one who sailed was excused from housework, light or otherwise. The cook did not have to wash dishes, though he was perfectly welcome to do so if he desired.

They saw the sun rise that morning, and it was shedding its last glowing rays over the restless waters when they made the harbor of St. Joseph's Bay. "Eighty miles in one day is not bad going for a 30-foot boat," said Ransom exultantly after measuring the charts.

"Sure not," chimed in Arthur. "If we could do that every day, the rest of the cruise would be an easy thing."

"Let's see," said Frank, counting on his fingers. "Eighty miles a day for 30 days would be 2,400 miles. At that rate we have only got about two months' more cruising, including stops."

"I hate to obstruct this beautiful two-month trip, but think of yesterday and add a couple of months." Kenneth, in his usual matter-of-fact manner, was throwing cold water upon these extravagant dreams.

St. Joseph's Bay, a deep indentation in the coast, afforded the young sailors a splendid anchorage, sheltered and easy of access. The rollers beat steadily on the beach outside, the roaring proclaiming the majesty of the sea. But within all was calm and still; gentle rollers rocked the yacht just enough to soothe, and the three youngsters slept like hibernating bears.

The soft breeze hummed gently through the rigging, the little waves lapped caressingly against the boat's sides, fishes bumped their noses inquiringly against her bottom. *His Nibs*, made fast by a long painter, went on little excursions of its own as far as the line would reach, like an inquisitive dog; but the boys slept through it, perfectly unconscious of all the interesting nocturnal goings on. It was not until the warm sun came shining through the port lights, and upon the open hatch, that they finally woke up.

"Seven bells, boys! Up, all hands, rise and shine—shake a leg!" Kenneth shouted, rubbing his own eyes to pry them open. It was seven o'clock and a long day's sail to Appalachicola was before them. Each boy, as he rolled out of his bunk, shook off the few clothes he had on and flopped overboard. In a minute, the sleepy dust was washed out of their eyes and the boys sported about like seals in the clear, warm salt water.

Frank climbed on deck and dove off, making a clear, arching leap like a hunted fish; but his feet had hardly disappeared before his head showed above the surface again.

"Why, you couldn't sink in this water if a millstone were hung around your neck," he spluttered, shaking the water out of his eyes.

Through St. George's Sound—a piece of water something like the Santa Rosa, separated as it is from the Gulf by a narrow strip of sand—they sailed to Appalachicola, then on along the harborless coast to Cedar Keys. It was a piece of sailing that Kenneth dreaded. The long, curving strip of coast without one adequate shelter along its entire length was not pleasant to think of in connection with an onshore gale. Kenneth examined the charts as the yawl sailed along, and noticed that the water was very shoal far from shore.

"How deep do you suppose it is off here?" he called up to Frank, who was steering.

"I don't know; it must be pretty deep, for we are five or six miles from shore," Frank answered. "But I can see bottom just the same; look at that seaweed waving as if the breeze was blowing on it. How deep is it, anyway?"

"Well, you may not believe it,"—Kenneth rolled up the chart and started aft to show the helmsman—"but it's only seven or eight feet. Pretty near as flat as a floor; about a foot a mile drop, I estimate."

"Why didn't we walk?" suggested Arthur, "as the Irishman said, when he saw the river coming up out of the water at Ellis Island."

They anchored that night about five miles from shore in seven feet of water, and the treacherous old Gulf was as calm as a park lake under a summer zephyr.

All the next day a roaring wind from the northwest wafted the three along, and night saw them safely anchored off the mouth of the Suwanee River. A star-studded sky hung over them as all three boys came out on deck after all was snug and shipshape. Kenneth got out his guitar, and to the accompaniment of its softly strummed chords, the boys sang: "Way down upon the Suwanee River, far, far away...."

The spell of the quiet was on them all, and as the sounds of their young voices died away and only the hum of the strings, the lap of the rippling water and the soft whir of the breeze were in their ears, a feeling of sadness came over them as they realized that they were indeed far, far from home.

Arthur lay flat on his back, gazing up into the immeasurable sky; Frank lay along the rail, looking into the clear, black, velvety depths of the ever-shifting water. Kenneth, absorbed in his brown study, watched the bow of the small boat abstractedly as the sharp stem cleaved the current of the tide, making little waves that glowed with phosphorescence.

For a while, no word was spoken, then "Phew!" snorted Frank. "I knew this was too good to last. What have we run up against, a fertilizer factory?"

"I thing doe," answered Arthur, holding his nose.

"Dee! Did it wordt thad a dead rat!" Ransom had his nostrils closed also, as his manner of speech indicated.

The stench drove the three boys into the cabin where, with closed doors and hatch, they sweltered until a shift of wind made it possible for them to breathe the outer air again. They looked in the direction from which the odor had come and saw the anchor light of a vessel swinging. Then, as their eyes became accustomed to the darkness, they made out the deeper shadow of the vessel herself.

Not until morning did they find out that the fragrance came from a sponge schooner. Though they hesitated some time, at last their curiosity overcame their squeamishness and, after washing down decks, breakfasting and cleaning up, Arthur and Frank (Kenneth having drawn the short yarn, as usual) took *His Nibs* and rowed over to the schooner. Kenneth watched his comrades from the *Gazelle* and saw them row very gingerly up to the trim vessel until the small boat's stem almost touched the larger boat's side. They half turned to go away but, evidently gathering up their resolution, they hailed a man on deck and went aboard.

Later Ransom himself had a chance to investigate the work. As he climbed the schooner's sides he found sponges of many sizes and shapes strung around the rigging in various degrees of decomposition. A big, West Indian Negro explained to him that they were hung up to rot the animal matter out of the fibrous substance which made the home of the multitude of small creatures. A very unsavory occupation, but one that pays quite well, the big fellow told Kenneth, and invited him to go sponge-fishing with him.

Ransom accepted and, getting into a small boat, they rowed some distance from the schooner. Putting a long, slender pine pole with a hook on one end into the boy's hands, the older man suggested that he try his luck. "This is easy," Kenneth said to himself as he slipped it into the water and began to feel about on the bottom. Soon the end struck something soft, and with a little thrill that always comes to the fisherman when he gets hooked to something, he began to haul up, slowly and carefully.

Under instructions from his host, he pulled up inch by inch. The thing he had on his hook was a dead weight, utterly unlike the active fish, but he thought that he detected a tremor in even this inert mass. Slowly and more slowly he raised the pole until he could dimly see a yellow-brown substance through the sunlit water. At last his catch was almost on the surface when the man began to laugh loudly.

"What's the joke?" Kenneth began, then stopped as he caught a clear glimpse of his treasure trove. An enormous mouth gaped at him and two protuberant eyes that shone like jewels gleamed in the sunlight, and a brown, flat body covered with warts and excrescences of various kinds flopped feebly on the surface. "Holy smoke, what have I struck?" Kenneth exclaimed, feeling that he had a waking nightmare. The thing slid off the hook and, scaling down through the water, was soon lost to view.

"Ugh!" said the boy, shivering in remembrance. "What was that?!"

"Angle-fish, I reckon. Scare yer?" the other replied.

Though Kenneth tried again, he could not haul up a sponge. There was a knack to it that completely baffled him.

All through this part of the Gulf, the boys found the sponge fishermen and their crews, many of whom were West Indians—great, big, strong fellows, who seemed to find the odoriferous life healthy. The shallow water, smooth and clear, produced good sponges, and the fishermen came to reap the harvest from all directions.

Even in the town of Cedar Keys, the boys could not get away from the horrid odor. The town, formerly a great cedar-producing place and the site of a large pencil manufactory, had become the sponge fishermen's port of call.

"For heaven's sake, Ken, let's get our mail, our grub and our water, and clear out of this place," Arthur said, the afternoon that they entered Cedar Keys Harbor. "It seems to me that sponge is mixed up with everything I eat, drink, smell, taste, see and touch. It's awful!"

"I'm willing," the skipper answered, "if Frank votes aye."

"Aye! Aye!" Frank shouted emphatically, with no loss of time.

Soon after dawn the next day, the mudhook was pulled up and the *Gazelle* stood for the open Gulf. She sped along as if she, too, were glad to get away into the free, sweet air of the southern sea.

It was a six-day sail to Charlotte Harbor, a little below Tampa, a sail full of incident: friendly races with fishing boats, exhilarating bouts with sharp little squalls that called for quick work and unerring judgment, and an entrancing view of an ever-changing semi-tropical coast.

A schooner with which they had been sailing hour after hour headed into the harbor, which opened up invitingly before both vessels.

"We might as well go in, too," suggested Ransom. "There's plenty of water and we might take a chance at a turtle or two. What do you say?"

So they rounded the lighthouse and sailed up the channel with their companion ship, like a team of horses. Together the jibs came down, and together the anchor chains rattled through the chocks. They learned from the lighthouse keeper that turtles were plentiful at this time of year, and that they crawled up on the beach at night to lay their eggs.

All three boys wanted to go, but one had to stay and keep ship, so after supper they drew lots.

"This yarn-pulling business is getting to be a sort of one-sided joke," declared Ransom aggrievedly. "I believe the strand I choose gets shorter when I take it."

"Hard luck, old man," Arthur and Frank said sympathetically, as they got into the small boat and pushed off.

Kenneth watched the boat as it skimmed the placid water, a dim shadow in the deepening gloom, and listened to the rhythm of the dipping oars and creaking rowlocks with a sense of loneliness that he found hard to shake off. The boat finally disappeared in the darkness and the sounds faded into the general murmur of the water. Soon a light showed on the beach and went swinging along, eclipsed at regular intervals by the legs of the carrier. The boys had lighted the lantern and, shouldering their guns, were on their way to the turtles' haunts.

Ransom wrote his log and finished some letters, then, taking some pillows on deck, was soon lulled to sleep by the soft wind and the gentle swing of the waves.

Loaded down with hatchets, guns and revolvers, Frank and Arthur looked as if they were on a pirating expedition; they went prepared for whatever might turn up. Bears are fond of turtle eggs and coons dote on them, so there was a reasonable chance of the boys' interrupting somebody's feast.

Side by side they walked, talking in low tones; both felt the tingling excitement that goes with hunting adventures day or night.

Once Frank caught sight of a dark something flopping in the water just beyond the tiny breakers and, half wild with excitement, he took up his rifle and shot at it. Arthur raised the lantern and they saw that it was a small shark caught in the shoal water.

"One on you, old man," laughed Arthur. "Think it was a sea serpent?"

After walking an hour or more, they rounded the point that protected the harbor, and were soon treading the sand of the outer beach.

"This must be the place," whispered Arthur. They walked more cautiously, looking for the parallel trenches in the sand that they had been told marked the passage of the giant turtles.

The damp salt air blew into their faces, made the flame of the lantern flicker and cast uncouth shadows on the sloping beach.

"There's one!" cried Arthur, giving his companion a grip on the arm. "Look!" And they both started on a run for the dark object that lay so still.

"Oh, come off! Don't you know the difference between a patch of sand grass and a green turtle? What about the laugh this time?"

"That's all right; I know a shark when I see it. This lantern flickers— By Jove! look at that!" Arthur stopped in his tracks and grabbed the light out of Frank's hand.

There were two deep tracks in the sand that paralleled each other—unmistakable signs of a monster turtle. Both boys followed the trail on the run, only to find that Madam Turtle had been and gone, also that bruin or coon had feasted royally on the eggs.

A hundred yards further on, they came to another track, and with excitement less strong, but still with nerves and muscles tense and hearts throbbing, they followed fast. The moon broke from the clouds and silvered the crescent sea, the wind-tossed palms showed black against the sky and the beach shone white under the light. "Hurrah!" Frank shouted. "Now we can see." The pale gleam showed a dark shape ten yards from them that moved awkwardly. "There she is, Art. Come on!"

In a minute they had come up to a giant turtle which on their approach drew in its head, then shot it out again, its beaked mouth opening and closing wickedly.

"Shoot it, Frank!" Arthur cried, utterly flustered. "Hit him in the eye! Hit him somewhere, quick!"

"No, let's get hold of her shell and flop him over on his back, then we've got him." Taking hold of the huge creature's shell just back of the crooked hind legs, they heaved and strained to turn her over. It was no use, the beast was too heavy and the turtle, objecting to this treatment, started for the water.

"Shoot it, Frank! It'll get away!"

Frank did as he was bid, but the bullets had no apparent effect—the great creature waddled on even faster than before.

Arthur, almost beside himself with excitement, jumped onto the broad, rounded back, yelling and whooping, and swaying to and fro in his efforts to keep his balance on the living platform. Then, suddenly realizing that he held a hatchet in his flourishing right hand, he reached forward and struck it deeply into the snake-like skull.

LOST ON CAPTIVE ISLAND

Charlotte Harbor was so flooded with moonlight that the little wind ripples shone like frosted silver. The *Gazelle*, lying peacefully at anchor, floated like a shadow on the placid water.

Kenneth lay asleep on the cabin roof where he had moved from the more cramped position in the cockpit. Soundly as a tired man should, he slept. Then, disturbed by dreams of battles with wind and wave, he stirred, working his arms and legs like a dog who has visions of the chase. At first he moved uneasily but still lay in the same position; then, still dead asleep, began to work over to the yacht's rail.

A long, strong roller came in from the Gulf and rocked the yawl so that the deck sloped sharply. There was a sudden great splash and then all was still, the ripples circling away from the agitated spot. Suddenly the waters began to show signs of a struggle below, and an instant later a bedraggled white figure splashed to the surface and began spouting and spluttering. Kenneth coughed and wheezed as he got rid of a large quantity of warm salt liquid, and between gasps called himself all the names his water-soaked brain could think of. He finally pulled himself up on deck—rather weakly—and lay down in the cockpit to rest a minute.

"Well, I'll be jiggered. If that wasn't the greatest fool stunt! I am mighty glad the other fellows were not around. I should never have heard the last of it." He turned to go below and, as he did so, he heard the far distant crack of a rifle.

"Must be something doing with the turtles," he thought.

. . . . .

The rifle shot which Ransom heard was fired by Frank at the great turtle which, in spite of the hatchet in its skull and the boy on its back, was making for the sea, determined to escape. The hatchet, half buried in the thick bone, had no more apparent effect upon it than the dropping of an oyster shell on it would have had.

"Shoot him again, Frank!" shouted Arthur from his perch. "We've got to stop him."

The boy took careful aim at the sinister black eye, the only vulnerable spot visible, and fired. With a heave that threw Arthur from his feet, the great creature made its last struggle for freedom, throwing the sand in showers and digging great holes in the course sand. Then, folding its legs and tail beneath its roof-like shell, it died.

For a minute, the victors gazed at their victim; then, wiping away an imaginary tear of regret, went to search for eggs. In a hollow near the spot where the hunters had found Madam Turtle, they unearthed her eggs, several dozen of them. The boys put them in a canvas bag which they carried and went on to hunt for more shellbacks.

Before long they came again upon the telltale tracks in the sand and found a turtle at the end of them, smaller, but even more active than the first.

With great difficulty they managed to get a long piece of driftwood under the shell and, with the aid of this leverage, "end her over." Frank and Arthur immediately rushed forward to end her misery and received a shower of sand in their faces that nearly blinded them. They retired out of range in confusion and dug the sand out of eyes, ears and mouths. With powerful, sweep-like strokes, the turtle clawed the beach in its efforts to right itself, and scooped the sand until it had dug holes for each of its four legs, so deep that the coarse grains were beyond its reach, and it lay helplessly sprawling.

With a single hatchet stroke, turtle number two was dispatched and the victors sat a minute beside their game to rest.

"Gracious! I'd like to have these turtles in Chicago," remarked Frank with speculative instinct. "Just think of the gallons of green turtle soup they would make; and it cost 25 cents a half-pint plateful! Holy smoke, we would be millionaires in no time."

"But what are we going to do with them now?" Arthur had a way of coming down to realities with a sickening thud.

As if in answer to the question, the lighthouse keeper came towards them out of the fast-brightening dawn and showed them how to dismember the creatures. Taking two great hams, the two boys slung them on a pole stretched between them and started back to the place where they had left *His Nibs*.

The pieces of turtle meat, the guns, lantern and bag of eggs made such a heavy load that they were glad enough when they reached the spot where they had left the small boat. Arthur and Frank looked out over the water and saw the *Gazelle* swinging at anchor, glorified in the warm colors of the sunrise.

"What's the matter with Ken?" Frank exclaimed, pointing with his gun barrel at the figure on the yacht's deck, who waved and gestured frantically.

"He is pointing at something. What's the matter with the chump? He is shouting." Arthur stopped to listen. The faint sound of a voice came over the harbor, but they could not make out what it said.

"He is pointing." Arthur was shading his eyes and looking intently. "What in the name of common sense is— By George, look at *His Nibs*." Arthur was pointing now at the little boat which, like a mischievous youngster, was bobbing about airily a short distance from shore.

"Jove! It's well we came along when we did. That little tub would have been out to sea in a minute."

As it was, Arthur had to swim for it, and only caught the truant after a long race. "The next time I leave you alone," he said as he pulled himself over the stern, "I am going to make you fast to a ten-ton anchor."

It was a merry feast that the reunited three enjoyed that morning. Turtle steak, which Kenneth declared to be equal to porterhouse and much like it in flavor, was the piece de resistance; but the talk and chaff were the garnishes that made the meal worthwhile.

"You have got to wash dishes, old man," Kenneth said to his mate when every vestige of the breakfast had disappeared, "while Frank and I get this old houseboat underway." And he sang lightly as he went on deck:

"*Gazelle, Gazelle,*
She'll run pell-mell
With every stitch a-drawing;
O'er waters smooth,
And waters rough,
The seas her forefoot spurning."

Soon Arthur heard the cheep, cheep of the halyard blocks as the mainsail was hoisted, then the metallic clink of the ratchet on the capstan. Frank's cry, "She's broke!" was followed by the swift whir of the jib halyards hauled taut and the creak of the blocks as the mainsail was sheeted home. Then the slap, slap of the little waves against the yacht's sides as she heeled to the fresh breeze told Arthur that they were underway again.

"There's no use talking, this beats farming," Arthur said to himself. "But, Jerusalem, we had it hard on the Old Mississippi. I don't hanker for any more of that."

After getting underway, the order came: "All hands and the cook prepare meat." There was a large amount of turtle meat left that was too valuable to be wasted. The flesh was cut up into strips, thoroughly sprinkled with salt and hung up in the rigging where the sun shone full upon it, to dry. It was not a very appetizing job, nor did the yacht herself present a very attractive appearance, but the product turned out all right. Turtle meat and turtle eggs were on the bill of fare for some time.

Kenneth made the unsavory remark that if the meat-preserving experiment proved a failure, the *Gazelle* would be about as fragrant as a sponge-fishing boat.

After a four-hour run, Frank, who climbed up into the port rigging, glass in hand, made out Captive Island, a low-lying strip of land that just showed above the surface of the water.

As they drew nearer, they could see that it was densely wooded—palms tossed their feathery heads, the great live oaks stretched out their sturdy arms mightily, and here and there a cedar stood out black in contrast with the lighter greens.

"I'd like to explore that island," said Arthur. "What's the matter with laying off there for the night?"

"All right; harbor is good and water enough," Kenneth admitted after looking at the charts.

The anchor was let go into three fathoms, off a sort of rude landing which, they later found, was built by a man who lived on the island and raised vegetables for the northern market.

After supper Frank and Arthur went ashore but soon returned, driven away by mosquitoes. Frank declared that he had seen enough of that place at close quarters and that if the skipper and Arthur wanted to explore, he was satisfied to stay and tend ship.

"Why, " said he, "except where the fellow has his vegetable patch, the whole place is a morass right down to the water's edge. I guess there is a beach on the Gulf side, now I think of it."

"That's it—that beach! That's what I want to explore." Arthur was of an investigating turn of mind.

It was unnecessary to go through the usual plan of drawing lots to determine who should go and who should stay. Frank stuck to his previous statement that he would not go "chasing 'round in that miserable mud hole." After all the morning's work was done, the skipper and the mate got into *His Nibs* and rowed off.

The little landing was a primitive affair, hardly strong enough, the two boys thought, to allow for very heavy shipments being made from it; but it was sufficiently sturdy to bear their weight without a tremor. From it led a path through tilled land, green with the young shoots of a freshly planted crop.

Kenneth and Arthur followed this road for some distance. Fields crowded it closely on either side; then it branched and the boys found themselves walking on a narrow strip of solid ground, hemmed in on both sides by a morass so deep and uncanny that they shivered. Tall palmettos grew out of the slimy ground, and vines twisted around in every direction like thin, green serpents. Gray moss hung from the branches everywhere like veils placed to hide some ghastly mystery. The path was well trod and firm, and the two boys, feeling that it must lead somewhere, went on quickly. For an hour they traveled through the swamp, winding in and out among the trees wherever the earth was firm.

"I wonder if this is another case of 'Lost in the Dismal Swamp,'" said Arthur, whose looks belied his cheerful tone.

"No, this path is perfectly clear. It will be easy enough to get back if we want to," Kenneth replied. "Getting cold feet?"

"No, sure not. But I would like to get out into the open, all the same."

The thick trees shut out all the breeze there was, and the damp, currentless air was heavy with the odors of decaying vegetation. Perspiration was running down the boys' faces, and spots of dampness began to show on the backs of their white jumpers.

"Hurrah!" shouted Kenneth. "There's the beach."

A rift in the trees showed the blue sky, and the invigorating sound of surf reached their ears. Soon they came upon a stretch of sand that shone white under the morning sun—smooth and hard and clean as a newly-swept floor.

In a minute the two were running races up the beach that stretched before them like a straight-away track. They ran and frolicked from the pure joy of living. Under the clear sky and shining sun, they forgot the gloomy forest and the stagnant marsh. Not until they were all out of breath did the rollicking skipper and his undignified mate stop to rest. Then they stretched at full length on the clean sand and gave themselves up to the joys of doing nothing, when there was no need to work under the stress of an exacting conscience.

Neither of the boys realized how long they had lain there, supremely comfortable as they were, until the pang of hunger began to make itself felt.

"Look at that, Ken," Arthur exclaimed, pointing to the sun long past the meridian. "Why, it must be afternoon."

"My stomach feels like it," the other admitted. "Better be going back, I guess."

They got themselves up and began walking leisurely along the beach, stopping now and then to pick up a shell or to dip their bare feet in the up-running waves.

"This is the place, Ken," said Arthur, turning to two tall palmettos growing on the edge of the forest.

"No, that isn't it," the other replied. "There was a crooked cedar near the path where we came out."

"I bet it's the place," Arthur said positively. "Let me prove it to you."

When they reached the trees, they glanced beyond them and saw the thick, black ooze of the morass. A pale fungus thrust out of the mud here and there added to the dismal aspect of the place.

"Ugh!" Arthur shivered.

"I told you so," Kenneth jeered, "not a sign of a path."

They walked on, looking for the crooked cedar, but not one could be seen. Everywhere were palmettos, straight and tall, swaying in the breeze and beckoning like sirens luring them to the destruction that lurked just beyond.

Every little opening that looked as if a path might lead from it was searched eagerly, but the black swamp always stared them in the face whenever they looked beyond the first line of trees. Hour after hour they searched, at first hopefully, then doggedly, driven on by the feeling that they must do something—that if they hunted carefully enough and persistently, the way would surely be found.

The sun sank lower and lower, and the feather-like fronds of the trees cast longer and longer shadows over the beach; still the boys searched for the elusive path. Thirst was added to ravenous hunger that increased every minute. The long walk through the woods and, later, the almost continuous exposure to the sun, had brought on a longing for water that was getting well-nigh unbearable.

"What fools we were not to mark the trees where we came out," Kenneth wailed as they dropped down on the sand, worn out. "We were so glad to get out of the place that we did not think about getting through again."

"We can't go around," Kenneth said, thinking aloud. "The swamp comes right down to the water on all sides of the island but this. I guess we have got to stick it out all night, old man." Kenneth laid his hand on his friend's shoulder.

"My, but I'm thirsty!" was the mate's only comment.

With a suddenness peculiar to the tropics, the sun went down in a blaze of color, and in its stead came a cloud of mosquitoes, bloodthirsty and poisonous. Without protection of any kind the boys suffered terribly—faces, hands and feet were soon covered with the itching little spots, which spread until their whole bodies were covered with the bites of the pests. Their thirst increased until their mouths seemed like dry ovens lined with dust and cracked with heat. Hunger, too, assailed them—the hunger of healthy appetites long unappeased, gnawing and weakening.

Kenneth gathered some half-green wood from the edge of the forest, built a fire, and in the dense smoke they sat as long as they could, or until they choked.

Then, in order that one, at least, might rest, they took turns in brushing the invading mosquitoes from each other. While one rested the other plied a palm branch; and so they passed the long night, interminable as it seemed.

At length the gray dawn began to steal over the sea, and the boys, weak with hunger and almost frantic with parching thirst, thanked God for it. They knew that with the appearance of the sun the mosquitoes would go, and, with hope that "springs eternal," they longed to begin the search for the path again.

Soon the heavens were lighted with the glory of the sunrise, and the waters, tinged with its colors, heaved and tossed like a great surface of iridescent molten metal—constantly changing, showing new shades that ran into one another, dimpled, flamed and faded.

Arthur and Kenneth could appreciate the beauty of the scene in a dull sort of way only. They suffered terribly; the pangs of hunger and the tortures of thirst drove all else from their minds. A plunge in the cool surf, however, refreshed them greatly, though it took all their resolution to resist the temptation to drink the intensely salt water.

As they were about to begin their search anew, they noticed a little black dog trotting about near the edge of the woods. The boys were very much pleased to see the little beast. He was frisky and well fed—evidently the pet of some household—and the two lost ones were glad of even this remote connection with civilization.

Kenneth suddenly made an exclamation; he tried to whistle also, but his parched lips would not admit of it.

"I've got an idea, Art. Listen."

Arthur stopped trying to make friends with the little visitor.

"That dog got here somehow; he must have come along some

path, and he will know the way back. We have got to make him go home, then we will follow. See?"

Arthur did see, and changed his tactics accordingly. "Go home!" he shouted. But the dog suddenly grew very friendly, wagged his tail and came trotting across the sand towards them. It was most exasperating. "Go home!" both shouted at once, and waved their arms menacing. The dog evidently thought it some kind of a game, and he frolicked about as if it were the greatest fun imaginable. "That won't do," muttered the older boy, and he stooped as if to pick up a stone. This was an old game that the dog fully understood. Many a time had he chased a stick into the water. He danced about and barked joyfully.

"There, you miserable little critter, go home!" Kenneth threw a pebble that struck just before the dog's nose, and he stopped in astonishment. Another well-directed stone changed his doggie joy and confidence to fear and, lowering his tail, he began to slink towards the woods and the swamp.

The boys' hearts beat high with hope, though they felt ashamed to treat such a friendly little beast so unkindly. A well-feigned angry shout and threatening gestures were enough to make their involuntary friend turn tail and run for home. Once started, he ran in earnest. Fearful that they would lose sight of him before he showed the path, the boys rushed after, panting and almost fainting with hunger and thirst. Once they thought that they had lost their guide and their hearts sank but, in a minute or two, they saw him enter the woods and they carefully marked the place so that they were able to follow without trouble. The entrance was a most unlikely place, and they had passed it many times, but soon they saw clearly a well-beaten path leading through the maze of tree trunks and veiling moss.

With hearts full of thankfulness they followed along, faint, dizzy and well-nigh exhausted, but hopeful and happy once more. At no great distance they came to a comfortable plantation house, and there in the front yard—blessed sight!—was a well with tin dipper hanging on the pump box. The water, cool and clear, was the most delicious thing that they had ever tasted, and the remembrance of that draught of plain well water would always linger with them. As they drank, their canine friend eyed them from behind the corner of the house and, though they did their best to show their gratitude, he mistrusted and would have none of them.

After thanking the good people of the house they went on and at last reached the landing. It took nearly all their remaining strength to row out to the *Gazelle*, and though Frank plied them with questions showing the effects of his long night of worry, they could hardly answer him intelligently until he had strengthened them with black coffee and some food.

As soon as the skipper and mate had recovered their strength, they weighed anchor and sailed away from the island that had so nearly been the scene of their death.

Down the coast they sped, nearer and nearer the long point that divides the Gulf of Mexico from the Atlantic Ocean. The boys grew more and more impatient as they drew gradually nearer to the ocean. The stops were as brief as possible; they merely paused to get fresh water and buy fruit or necessary food. There were no towns of interest to visit—mere clusters of fishermen's huts.

Cape Romano, that point around which the waters of the Gulf continually froth and rage, was passed in safety, though the *Gazelle* tossed about roughly and had, for a time, a tussle with the seas that tested her thoroughly.

Now began the trip through that maze of intricate channels of the Ten Thousand Islands, where many a good vessel has been lost—a place that was once the refuge of pirates, and even now retains the flavor of bloodthirsty tales. On one of these islands, or keys, the boys landed in search of fresh water. After walking a while, they came to a snug little cove or inlet and were surprised to find a graceful sloop anchored cozily therein. From the cove led a well-beaten path, which, Frank and Kenneth following, came to a picturesque cottage thatched with palm branches. It was weather-beaten but looked comfortable.

A young woman was standing in front and, in answer to their polite questions about water and the easiest of the many puzzling channels to follow, suggested that they ask "John," and pointed with her thumb over her shoulder to the open door of the hut. Needing no second invitation, their curiosity fully aroused by the strange remoteness of this little home, they stepped in and looked through the door into the larger of the rooms the house contained.

There, prone on the floor, stretched on a gray rag carpet, lay an old man. His complexion was brown, dark and rich in color as century-old mahogany. His thick, white hair—bushy and plentiful—framed a face seamed and lined, but keen and full of vigor. The old man stirred at the sound of the boys' steps, then rose and went toward them inquiringly.

"The young lady said that you knew all about the coast and could tell us the best way to get through the islands," Kenneth began.

"Yes, I do know something of the coast," and the old man smiled, as if at a joke too private to be told.

He asked the boys about themselves, and was much interested in their tale of pluck and their plans for the balance of the cruise. After they had finished their recital, he, in his turn, began an account of the channels, harbors, shoals, tides and currents, that showed an acquaintance with the coast along the Gulf that was indeed marvelous. His voice was clear and full, and he gestured freely as he talked with the animation of a young man.

Both of the boys instinctively understood that there was something extraordinary about him, although they could not tell what it was.

He expressed a wish to see the boat that had been built so far away from the warm clime she was now visiting, so the youngsters filled their breaker at a spring near the cottage and led the way to the beach where they had landed. It was quite a long walk, but the old native tramped it as sturdily as the young men themselves. The *Gazelle* lay swinging idly at her anchor, a sight to make her owner's heart glad.

The old man seemed much pleased with the yacht and complimented her builder. Then he talked about boats in general, displaying such a knowledge of vessels of all kinds that Kenneth's curiosity finally overcame him, and he asked if their host would not tell him some incident that they might put down in the log in remembrance of the visit—hoping that he might in some way reveal his history.

"Well, boys, how old should you say I am?" He looked quizzically from one to the other. Frank guessed 80; Kenneth 85, and he was afraid he was stretching it.

"Well, said he, "my name is John Gomez, and if I live 'til Christmas, as I hope I shall, I'll be 123."

Frank and Kenneth could do nothing but gaze at him open-mouthed. "Holy smoke!" at last exclaimed Frank.

"Now there's something to put down in your log," said John Gomez. "Good luck to you." He shook the boys' hands with a hearty grip and went off.

"Well," said Frank, as he and Kenneth got aboard *His Nibs* and pushed off, "a hundred twenty-three, think of it! I bet that old chap has a history."

And he had.

FIGHTING A MAN-EATING SHARK

It was some time before the boys heard about old John Gomez, but the tales that were current from Mobile to Key West would fill a book. According to one story, he was the only surviving member of a pirate crew, one of the many that formerly had cruised about in the waters of the Gulf of Mexico and the Caribbean Sea.

The crew of this ship had a disagreement about the division of the spoils, and a great fight followed. All but Gomez were slain, and though he was badly wounded, he hid the great treasure which was in his hands so carefully that no one had ever been able to learn its whereabouts. The old man had never alluded to the subject, and it was feared that his secret might die with him. Some said that the young woman the boys saw with the old man was a relative; others declared that she was merely a guard stationed to secure the secret should the centenarian by any chance let it drop unawares.

Gomez's general appearance did more than a little to give credence to these stories: His looks were certainly of the piratical order—a lean, sallow face, keen, piercing black eyes, gold rings in his ears and a watchfulness that never wearied were characteristics which he had in common with light-fingered gentlemen of seafaring tastes.

Over a year later the boys read a newspaper clipping describing his death. He was drowned while sailing alone in his sloop on the open Gulf. But they never heard if any of the treasure had been found.

For several days the voyagers travelled among the Ten Thousand Islands, winding in and out through the labyrinthine channels. It was a journey full of incident. Islands of every size and shape, green islands and islands bare of verdure, crowded the sea.

A whole week passed, and the boys did not see the least sign of a white man. Every vessel of sufficient size stood out into the Gulf to avoid the winding passages. They ran across several Seminole Indians, tall, splendid fellows, who considered the coils of bright-colored cloth on their heads sufficient covering for the whole body.

At last they sighted Cape Sable, and they knew that with a favorable wind the *Gazelle* would soon be ploughing the waters of the Atlantic Ocean. Off Cape Sable the *Gazelle* ran into a fleet of fishing boats, and for an hour the boys and men of the fishing boats swapped yarns; then they busied themselves laying in a stock of coconuts against future need.

It was a straight run from Cape Sable to Grassy Key, one in the long chain of islands which drip off the end of the Florida peninsula. At last only the narrow island lay between the *Gazelle* and the Atlantic Ocean. The great body of salt water Kenneth and his crew had so perseveringly fought to gain was almost in sight, and the deeper note of its thundering surf could at times be plainly heard. What might befall them on the greater tide they knew not, but with undaunted courage all were impatient to venture, and to learn.

The *Gazelle* reached her secure anchorage just as the storm, which had been threatening for several days, broke with terrible fury. Sheltered as they were, the joy of the boys at reaching the last obstacle to their way to the Atlantic gave place to awe as they heard the roar of the wind and felt the shock of the beating surf on the coral shores outside. For three days a heavy wind prevailed—too strong to allow of the *Gazelle* venturing out. In fact, the seas had been swept free of all craft as if by a gigantic broom. Then the boys were forced to live on an almost purely vegetable diet of coconuts and oatmeal—a liberal supply of weevils in the last constituting the only foreign element in the otherwise strictly vegetable nature of the food.

At the end of the three days, the wind subsided enough to allow the yacht to crawl out of her hole and, with wings spread wide, she entered the dangerous passage that led to the almost limitless waste of waters of the grand old ocean.

It was a proud moment for Kenneth when his yacht sailed out on the broad Atlantic—pride in his boat, pride in the crew and a pardonable satisfaction with his own good work.

"All hail to Old Ocean!" shouted the crew as the *Gazelle*, with a shake like the toss of the head, bounded into the embrace of the Atlantic's long billows.

"Well, we did it!" cried the mate exultantly. "Sailed to the ocean."

"And we will sail back, too," added Frank.

"But we have a trick or two to turn yet." Kenneth foresaw experiences before them during the long coast-wise trip.

The voyage up the Hawk Channel to Miami on Biscayne Bay seemed long only because of their short supply of food. When they anchored off that southernmost town on the mainland of Florida, they were ready to tackle anything in the shape of eatables except oatmeal and coconuts.

For many, many days the boys had not been able to send word to their people in far-off Michigan, nor had they heard from home. At Miami a big batch of mail awaited them, and they at once satisfied a hunger for home news and civilized food. Day by day the boys had added to their letters, until Uncle Sam received almost as much mail matter as he had brought.

For two days the boys enjoyed the comfort of a safe anchorage in a port, and all hands got a good rest, many good feeds and a good haircut apiece. When their unkempt shaggy locks were shorn, the places once protected from the sun showed white in contrast to their tanned skins.

"Arthur, you look like Barnum's piebald boy," said Frank, pointing a derisive finger at him.

"Well, you look as if you needed a good scrub. You started all right, apparently, but you must have got tired."

"Every man his own hair brush," said Ransom, running his fingers appreciatively through his stiff, closely cropped hair. "If I could only reach my feet with my head I would always have a

119

shine."

"That's all right; you can reach mine," and Arthur put his foot up to prove it.

The fame of the young sailors and their staunch craft had preceded them, so they made many friends in the far southern town, and spent the days very pleasantly. The place was a great shipping point for pineapples—crates of the spiky fruit were being shipped by the thousands to northern cities and now, for once in their lives, the boys had their fill of them—great, juicy, luscious things ripened in their own warm native sun.

In spite of all these enticements, Kenneth and his crew were eager to begin their long cruise up the coast, and in spite, also, of many invitations to stay, they weighed anchor and got underway the second day after they had entered the famous harbor. The bay, though large, was full of bars, and these and great masses of seaweed made it difficult to keep to the deep water.

A fine breeze was blowing and the *Gazelle*, her booms well to port, sailed off handsomely. Her crew, rested, well fed and at peace with all, were in high spirits and proud of the fine appearance their yacht made. Kenneth at the stick, Frank tending sheets, Arthur below making all snug for the coming tussle with the ocean—all were in high feather.

The *Gazelle* was sailing her best, skimming over the water at good speed like a graceful gull, when suddenly she struck bottom and stopped with a jar. There she stuck, all sails spread and every stitch drawing, but as hard on the bar as though she had been rooted to it. This was too common an experience to give the boys any uneasiness, but the delay was vexatious and they tried every means that experience suggested to shove her into deep water. The tide was falling, and they soon saw that there was nothing to do but wait until it changed to flood and released them. A long day of waiting was before them, and since with the falling water the yacht careened more and more, there was no comfort in staying aboard of her.

"What's the matter with a swim?" Frank suggested.

"I'll beat you in," Kenneth responded. In a trice, all three were overboard.

Farther on the bar was entirely bare, and a smooth, hard sand beach was left. One side sloped suddenly into deep water and made a splendid diving place.

For an hour the three swam in the warm salt sea, and then Ken and Arthur, growing a little weary of the sport, went on shore and lay basking on the beach. Frank, however, not satisfied, continued to float about.

Arthur and Kenneth talked comfortably for some time, then, becoming interested, fell into a lively discussion, which Arthur suddenly interrupted with, "Why, look at Frank. What in the world is the matter with him?"

"Oh, he's just fooling. Splashing around for exercise," Kenneth answered indifferently.

It was Frank's peculiar motions that had attracted Arthur's attention. He swam around in circles, then he stopped and splashed and made a great to-do. After that, he swam ahead for a little, only to stop and begin all over again his previous absurd tactics.

"He's not fooling, Ken; something is the matter with him. Perhaps he has got a cramp." Just as Arthur stopped speaking, Frank seemed to regain his senses and swam straight ahead in an entirely rational and dignified, if somewhat speedy fashion.

Then, all of a sudden, he began to lash about with arms and legs anew. His feet and hands flew about like flails and beat the water into white, foamy lather. The two boys watched the antics of their friend with growing alarm. All at once they saw something that stirred them to instant action: the sharp triangle of a shark's fin cutting through the water just behind Frank's wildly waving arms.

. . . . .

The water was delightful and Frank was not yet ready to come in when Arthur and Kenneth had had enough, so he dived over and swam out where the tide was several times over his head. Once he dived down and tried to reach bottom. As he rose toward the surface, his heart laboring for air, his face turned up, he saw a sinister shadow slowly swaying in the yellowish-green water almost above him. For an instant his heart sank and cold chills ran up and down his spine. Never had he seen so large a shark, and for a moment he almost lost his presence of mind. Then, with a rush, his courage returned and, working arms and legs with frantic zeal,

121

he shot up to the surface and began splashing about to frighten the shark off, a plan that he had heard was sometimes successful. For a while the man-eater, surprised by these tactics, was held at bay. Then, as Frank grew weary of his efforts and stopped to rest, the monster drew slowly nearer and began to turn on his back to allow his long, under-cut jaw to work.

"He'll have me in a minute," thought Frank, and he began a new movement. Turning suddenly, he swam *straight for the shark*, arms and legs going like miniature paddle-wheels. It was a bold move, and life or death depended on its success or failure. Straight at the ugly, cruel head he swam, and directly away from shore. For a moment the shark lay still, its fins slowly waving, its evil eye watching its enemy; the curved line of the wicked mouth was partly visible. Nearer swam the boy, nearer until he could almost feel the current set in motion from those powerful fins.

"I am a goner, sure," thought Frank, but he determined to play the game out to the end and kept on. Where were Kenneth and Arthur? Why did they not come to his rescue, he wondered, with a fearful dread at his heart.

Surely the shark was backing away from his onslaught. In spite of aching limbs and laboring lungs, the boy increased his efforts and followed after the retreating tiger of the sea. He had been struggling for a long time and his whole body ached with the exertion; he felt that he could not keep up much longer. Once when his mouth was open, gasping for breath, he had splashed it full of water and had had to stop a minute to cough it out. His heart was beating like a trip hammer, and each move seemed to take the last ounce of his strength.

The boy felt that he must give up, and wondered vaguely if a shark made quick work of a chap, and what his people at home would think of his end. Just as he seemed at the very last gasp, he felt the clutch of Kenneth's hand on his hair and the firm grip warm on his bare arm. Then, half dead with fatigue and dazed with horror, the limp figure was dragged into the small boat by Kenneth's sturdy arms.

Feebly, the exhausted boy was able to say, "You came in the nick of time, old man; I could not have lasted much longer."

Kenneth answered not a word, but thought with a shudder of

how close he had come to mistaking his friend's frantic movements for playful antics. He reached out his hand and grasped the other's fervently—it was a grip of thankfulness and affection on both sides.

Though Frank's escape was narrow, the recovery of his high spirits was almost immediate, and soon the three friends were running races on the exposed sandbar as if one of them had never been in peril of his life, let alone a short hour before.

With the returning tide the *Gazelle* straightened up, and after a few strong pulls on the anchor, which had been previously dropped for that purpose, she slipped off into deep water. It was still early afternoon, so with an eased sheet and light hearts the *Gazelle* and her gallant crew passed through the channel, out on the open ocean.

"Look at that old lighthouse; that's a fine tower, but I don't see any signs of a lantern." Frank pointed to a tall shaft like a great chimney that rose from a cluster of palm trees. The yacht was slipping past the long point that forms one of the barriers between the ocean and Biscayne Bay.

"That must be the old Cape Florida light a fellow in Miami told me about," said Ransom, gazing at the tall, graceful tower that pierced the blue.

"That tower has a story to tell. This place was full of Indians, I don't know how long ago, and the lighthouse keeper and his assistant, a colored man, were in mortal terror of them. They thought, however, that they had a safe refuge, if worse came to worst, in the tower. One day a big bunch of Indians came up and, after shooting a while at the men in the keeper's house, set it afire. To save themselves from being roasted alive, the two men took refuge in the lighthouse itself and climbed up the long, winding flights of wooden stairs to the lantern room on top. For a time it seemed as if they were safe, but the ingenious devils soon hit upon the plan of setting fire to the stairs and platforms inside the tower. The door open at the bottom and top, the lighthouse became a veritable chimney and the flames licked up the dry woodwork in a flash."

"Gracious! What happened to the men?" Frank interrupted Kenneth to ask.

"When it got too hot inside," Ransom continued, "and when the platform they were standing on inside began to smoke, they climbed out on that narrow little run-around outside; you can see it from here."

The skipper pointed to the tower and the little balcony running around it near the top.

"Phew! That would be an unpleasant place to stay with a fire burning in the tower inside and a lot of savages looking for your gore, hanging 'round waiting for you to drop off."

"But they didn't drop off," Kenneth went on. "They stuck to the little balcony 'til the Indians got tired waiting and began shooting at them with their bows and arrows. The men lay flat on the boards, as close to the bricks as they could get. But before long the assistant got an arrow through his heart and the keeper himself was shot in the shoulder. The Indians, thinking that both were done for, went away, leaving the wounded man with the dead one, high up on a lonely tower, the only means of reaching the ground burned away, without food, and entirely without shelter."

"Did he die up there?" both of the other boys inquired at once.

"Almost, but not quite. Some of the settlers near, fearing trouble, followed the Indians in force, and a daring chap climbed up the charred stumps of the supports inside the tower and lowered the body of the assistant and the almost lifeless keeper to the ground."

"What a story!" Frank shuddered as he looked at the tall shaft.

"But it's true. The place has never been used since. See, there's no sign of life there."

The boys watched the tower until it sank below the curve of the earth, and for a long time sat silent, thinking of the keeper's awful plight.

Rounding Cape Florida, the yacht sailed north along the treacherous east coast of Florida. With scarcely any harbor and a strong sea beating steadily on shore, the boys watched with dread for the "glistening calm," when the wind dies out suddenly, leaving a heavy sea setting in to shore. But luck was with them, and three days after leaving Biscayne Bay they had reached St. Lucie's inlet to Indian River and were standing off and on before the thundering breakers guarding the pass to the calm water beyond.

On the chart, laid out in beautiful lines, clear figures and delicate shadings, the course through those raging billows was plain enough to the haven beyond; but the real look of the place was very different.

"Well, boys, shall we do it?" Kenneth's mind was already made up, but he wanted the confirmation of his friends. "it's win out or bust, you know."

"The chart says that there's water enough. I am willing to risk it." Pluck was Frank's long suit, that was sure.

"Water enough? I should say so." Arthur gazed at the spouting breakers, which stormed the beach like ranks of white-plumed warriors. "I'm game, if Ken says so."

For answer, Kenneth shifted the helm and headed straight for the seething breakers.

Arthur went forward and clung to the rigging to watch for the channel markers, while Frank lay aft with the skipper to tend sheets and be handy for any emergency. The hatches were closed tight and all movable gear lashed down.

Like a war horse eager for the fray, the *Gazelle* dashed for the first line of tumbling watery breastworks. Rising like a gull on the uplift of the first wave, she topped it and swung down into its trough and then up the slope of the next. Straight as an arrow, steady and sure as the sweep of a true wind, the yacht slipped over the white crests of the great waves, one after the other, on through the narrow, troubled waters of the inlet, to the calmer waters of Indian River.

"Say, that was just great," was Frank's honest compliment to the boat's performance. "I'd like to do that again." The faces of all three were damp from the salt spray and shining with exhilaration and enthusiasm.

As Kenneth was about to drop his anchor, his eye caught sight of a queer-looking craft that was gliding over the smooth water in the rapidly deepening dusk.

"Let's travel along with our friend over there," he said, pointing to the strange vessel. "She may be able to give us some pointers about this creek."

The *Gazelle* was the faster sailer, and had just about come abeam of the stranger, when they heard her anchor go overboard.

The yawl's mudhook immediately followed suit. While Frank was getting the supper, the skipper and his mate rowed over to what proved to be a broad-beamed sharpie. After hailing, the boys were invited to come aboard by the one person visible. Climbing a ladder thrown over her square sides, the two found themselves in a very comfortable cabin lined with shelves, on which were ranged, in orderly rows, the stock of a well-appointed grocery store.

The skipper-proprietor was a jovial fellow, having the characteristics of both of his trades—a trader's Yankee shrewdness and love of gossip, combined with the open, hearty, yarn-spinning qualities of a sailor. He gave Ransom and his friend many useful hints about navigating Indian River, with tips on every shoal and indentation of which he was familiar, and ended by selling them quite a stock of provisions. "Combining business with pleasure," he said, as he handed Arthur the packages of flour, salt, sugar and coffee.

Next morning the two boats traveled along in company for a time. Then, as the sailor-grocer stopped to solicit a customer ashore, the *Gazelle* sped on alone.

Sailing along the queer, elongated, inland bay-like river was not an unmixed pleasure. A paradise for fishermen it was, as well as the haunt of mosquitoes with bills long and strong enough to "pierce anything and clinch on the other side." The crew was compelled to live in the smoke of burning, half-dried coconut husks at times; but when the captain could stand this no longer, he resorted to an invention of his own. Wrapping himself in a blanket up to his neck, Kenneth stuck his head into a large tin cracker box which he had pierced full of holes and draped with cheesecloth. Though it was like a continuous Turkish bath in the tropical weather, the skipper declared that it was better to steam than to be eaten alive.

To compel yachtsmen to make use of their services, the local watermen were in the habit of destroying the channel marks, so our sailors spent much time sounding out the deep water—a task which the hot sun and voracious mosquitoes made far from pleasant.

Mosquito Lagoon is reached from Indian River by what is

called Haul Over Canal, once in good repair, but when the *Gazelle* nosed her way to, she found that it was half-filled with sand and too shallow to allow her to pass through.

It was a question whether they would retrace their steps or dredge a deeper channel through the 60-foot-wide bar to the shortcut.

The discovery of the old blade of a cultivator among the junk of the ballast helped the boys to decide in favor of dredging a channel. For two days they worked, waist-deep in the water, the hot sun beating on their backs and necks, the mosquitoes humming a merry tune in their ears, and the stinging sea nettles, or jellyfish, irritating the skin of arms and legs. Added to these discomforts was the constant danger of being stung by the "stingaree," whose slightest touch means a poisoned wound and sometimes fearful suffering and death.

Game of all sort abounded in the lagoon. The waters teemed with brilliantly hued fish. Herons and flamingoes were frequently seen stalking about at a distance in their ridiculous disjointedly dignified fashion, while pelicans, their huge pouches distended with fish, were everywhere.

After leaving New Smyrna, which called itself the oldest town in the United States and proudly displayed an old mission to substantiate the claim, the yacht reached the ocean's outlet, an ugly place, through which the water rushed in never-ceasing fury. Jagged rocks fretted the water into foam in every direction. Blocking the channel at one side lay the boiler of a wrecked steamboat; beyond, the breakers roared as if hungry for their prey.

On the morning of the Fourth of July the *Gazelle* slowly approached the inlet, while her crew prepared for the struggle. With everything snug, rigging as taut as the nerves of the skipper and his crew, the gallant little ship swept to the battle.

A THRILLING FOURTH OF JULY CELEBRATION

With everything drawing, the *Gazelle* rounded the point which had obscured the view of the inlet, and her crew got the first clear sight of the danger they were so soon to encounter. There flowed the strip of water connecting lagoon with ocean, running out to the parent sea like a mill race, for the tide was on the ebb. When the racing current and the incoming breakers met, there was a crash that could be heard from an incredible distance; spray was hurled high in air, and the watery foes seemed to dash each other to vapor! To the left of the channel was the black dome of the boiler of a wrecked boat, blocking half the passage.

Right through this must the *Gazelle* go. Could she get past the huge, obstructing cylinder of iron? Would she live to get through those terrifying, battling seas? These questions each boy asked himself as the yacht, answering her helm, readily pointed her bowsprit straight for the opening. With "Old Glory" flapping at the peak in honor of Independence Day, she flew swiftly on. A good breeze was blowing, and, aided by the swift ebb tide, the good boat was soon in the midst of the fray.

On they sped, with wind and tide aiding, the *Gazelle* simply flying until she was well on her way in the vortex of the racing chute. Just before loomed the huge, round dome of the boiler, and the breakers warred beyond. All was going well, when suddenly the wind failed, and Kenneth, looking up to note the cause, saw the great sand dune that created a barrier to the friendly breeze. The yacht, carried by the tide alone, moved on until she reached the first roller, which struck her fairly forward, twisting her around so that she rolled in the trough of the sea.

The boys realized that if help did not come immediately, they were doomed to destruction, either by being dashed to pieces against the boiler, or by being carried broadside into the breakers and then being hammered to fragments. With no wind to give steerage way, they were utterly helpless.

Nearer and nearer the yacht drifted, nearer to encounter the two perils. The national ensign hung at the peak, limp and dispirited. Kenneth, watching it to see if some stray breeze might not straighten out its drooping stripes, wondered if their luck had failed them at last. All was done that could be done—the three youngsters were in the hands of Providence; and the skipper watched "Old Glory," dimly feeling that it was a sort of talisman that would bring rescue.

Nearer and nearer they drifted to the great iron dome; louder and louder sounded the surf. Then, a miracle! The flag moved as if stirred by an invisible hand, the outer corner flapped, the stripes straightened out, and the blue field of the jack stood flat—the succoring breeze had come! It was close work, but the *Gazelle* might yet be saved. If she could be got about in time she would just scrape the boiler and take the breakers head on.

With a warning cry to Arthur, who stood forward, Kenneth threw the helm hard over and the mate let go the jib. Swift and light as a dancer the good boat spun about, filled and streaked off on the other tack. Just clearing the boiler, she headed into the combing waves that rose high against the blue sky. For an instant she struggled against the rush of flying spume, her canvas drawing bravely; then she forged on, breasting the hill of water. For another instant she was enveloped in foam, then shaking herself free she dashed into the next, and so on to safety. Though drenched from masthead down, she rode the great seas to the rolling billows of outer ocean, and "Old Glory" snapped triumphantly at the peak.

Beyond the breakers all was plain sailing. The rollers were

high and long, but the great hill-like slopes were gradual, and the *Gazelle* coasted up and down them with a lightness and ease that suggested wings.

"Why don't we celebrate?" said Frank in an aggrieved tone.

Three rousing cheers and a tiger rang out in response, and several rounds were fired from the ship's miniature cannon, which made up in fuss what it lacked in feathers.

It was good to be sailing on the broad Atlantic where the sandbars and mosquitoes ceased to trouble. The water traversed was constantly changing. Inland sound succeeded open gulf, and boundless ocean followed inland waters. There was no danger of monotony, for the problems of navigation were constantly arising to the young navigators. Hour after hour the yacht sailed along, rising and falling on the swinging sea. The land was a mere irregular line on the horizon, which disappeared now and then as a rising hill of water hid it from the sight of the crew.

As the sun sank over the distant land, the clouds arose until they formed a black mass that shut out the light and cast a heavy gloom over all.

"We're in for the usual Fourth of July storm, I guess." The captain said, looking rather anxiously at the gathering clouds.

"Can we make harbor before it strikes us?" Arthur inquired.

"We'll try it," Kenneth answered, and suiting the action to the word, he eased his sheets and headed directly for shore.

The force of the wind increased as they drew nearer the shore; they were flying along in company with the scraps of water snatched from the wave crests. The clouds grew heavier and more dense, and the light fainter and fainter, until the boys could no longer make out the marks leading to harbor.

For a few minutes Kenneth held on the same course. Then, as the light drew dimmer and dimmer, and the wind gathered weight every minute, he wondered whether it would be possible to make harbor.

"We'll be on shore in a minute, and I can hardly make out that point now," the skipper said as he looked long into the gloom. "I would rather be out at sea than near an unknown coast with an onshore gale like this blowing. Are you with me, boys?

"Sure!" Arthur and Frank answered together in a single breath.

The *Gazelle's* helm was put down and she started in her fight to windward. Not until they faced the wind did the boys realize how hard it was blowing. The spray dashed into their faces cut like knives, and the roar was almost deafening. Slowly but steadily the *Gazelle* thrust her way into the wind and away from the thundering breakers.

Soon heaven's pyrotechnics began, and the boys on their wee chip of a boat, on an ocean dashed to foam, were treated to an exhibition of fireworks that overshadowed all the poor efforts of man to do honor to the nation's birthday. It was rather terrifying, but when the thunder ceased and the rain stopped, the air had such a clean, washed smell that the boys were glad to be out in it, though all hands were wet to the skin and the yacht's sails dripped like trees after a heavy rainfall. It was late when harbor was made, and all hands were glad enough when things were shipshape and they could turn in for the night, declaring each one from captain to cook that the Fourth had been fitly celebrated.

A few days later the *Gazelle* anchored off St. Augustine, that ancient city of the Spaniards and modern winter resort. Now it was deserted by its northern visitors, but it still hummed in a subdued sort of way, unexcited by the prospects of northern dollars. Kenneth and his friends found that even in summer the habit of charging three prices still clung to the people of the town, so they made haste to get away.

Straight out to sea the young mariners went, planning to make port at Fernandina, nearly on the line dividing Georgia and Florida. It was a longer run than the captain had anticipated, and it was nearly dark when they came near to "the haven where they would be."

"What do you say, boys," Kenneth inquired of his companions. "Shall we try for it?"

"It is getting pretty dark," suggested Frank. "Can't see the buoys marking the channel."

"That's right; look at the glass, Art."

"Going down like thunder," reported the mate emphatically.

"Let's try for it," said Arthur.

"I'd rather be in harbor if we are going to have another Fourth of July storm," Frank suggested, changing his ground.

"Well, I'm sorry to go against the judgment of you fellows, but I think that we had better stay outside than run up against a lot of shoals in the dark that we know nothing about."

The captain pronounced his opinion with the air of one who has considered the subject and has finally made up his mind. Though the other two disagreed with Kenneth, they had long ago realized that there must be a head to an expedition like this, and they were willing to abide by the skipper's judgment.

"All right, old man," Frank replied. "Shall I hang out the side lights?"

"Please. Light up the drug store." Frank winced at this ancient joke and went below to fill and trim the red and green lights.

The little 30-foot yacht with her precious freight continued her course out to sea in spite of the falling barometer and the almost absolute surety of a storm to come. It was surely a bold thing to do—many a skipper of a larger craft would have hesitated before going out upon the open ocean in the face of a storm at night when harbor was so close at hand. But Kenneth had absolute confidence both in the vessel he had so thoroughly tested and in the courage of his tried and true companions.

Not until midnight did the storm reach its height; then the "rains descended, and the floods came." The wind blew a fearful gale and the pitch blackness, rent at times by vivid lightning, closed in around the tossing yacht like a mighty hand.

Only those who have passed through one of the sudden storms which arise so frequently in those waters can have any idea of its vicious fury. The wind shrieked and the waves increased in power and volume, until the *Gazelle* sank out of sight behind them or was raised to a dizzy pinnacle from which she coasted down, her bowsprit pointing almost directly to the bottom. The wind-driven rain cut so that it was impossible to face it; and though the boys were clad in oilskins from closely tied sou'westers to bare ankles, the wet penetrated the seams, ran down their necks and drenched them through and through.

All hands were on watch that night; the hatches were battened down tight. They tried their best to keep to windward, but the tossing of the boat shook them around the narrow cockpit like dice in a box. Conversation was impossible; the wind snatched the words from their mouths and carried them out of hearing instantly. All was dark except for the fitful flash of lightning and the dim radiance of the binnacle lamp in Kenneth's face as he swayed over it to watch his course.

One, two, three hours passed, and the fury of the storm increased. It was a terrible strain on the young mariners, and each wondered in his inmost heart if they would come out of it alive. Somehow they did not fully believe they would. Battered and bruised, wet, chilled and utterly weary of buffeting with wave and wind, they clenched their teeth and by sheer force of will kept up their courage.

"What's that?" Kenneth's voice sounded weak and far off, but the accent was sharp and anxious for all that, and unmistakable.

There was a sharp crack that the three heard clearly above the howling wind and snarling sea. Something had parted, some vital part had given way. The *Gazelle* sailed less surely, she staggered up the steep sea slopes more heavily. Anxiously the three boys looked forward, upward, all around to find the cause. They dared not stand up to investigate; they could only look and long for a lightning flash to reveal the damage.

"There, look!" Frank shouted, and rose halfway to his feet, only to be dashed violently to the deck again.

A flash showed that the main gaff had broken in the middle, and was flapping heavily against the stout canvas of the mainsail.

The three boys stared at each other questioningly, though only an occasional flash of lighting revealed their faces. Each knew that something must be done—that unless the mainsail was lowered very soon it would be torn to tatters by the jagged ends of the broken gaff, or the broken spar banging around with the swaying of the yacht might injure some of the standing rigging and weaken the mainmast stays.

The tempest had not abated in the slightest, the wind still roared a gale, and the rain came down in a steady flood; the "sea rose mountains high."

"Take the stick, Arthur!" Kenneth made a funnel of his hands and roared to the mate. He had conceived a plan to reach the halyards at the foot of the mast and lower the broken stick. Hazardous as the plan was, it must be done.

Kenneth tied a stout line around his body and, taking a turn around a cleat close to the companionway, he gave the end to Frank.

"Pay out slowly, but be sure you keep a turn so that if I should go overboard you'll have me, see?" Kenneth shouted in his friend's ear. The other answered that he understood and grasped the skipper's arm a second, a gesture of devotion and confidence that conveyed a world of meaning.

Grasping the windward rail that ran around the roof of the cabin, Kenneth, flat on his face, began the perilous journey. It was scarcely 15 feet, a mere step, but a journey to the North Pole could hardly have been more dangerous. Crawling, creeping, rolling, the boy painfully made his way along. Frequently he was drenched with water and had to hold on to the slender rail with might and main. The wind beat the rain in his face; the motion of the yacht wrenched at his hands as if trying to make him let go. The broken gaff slatted and slapped over his head, threatening to fall and knock him senseless.

At length the plucky boy reached the mast and, shouting to Frank to let go the line, lashed himself securely to it. Arthur brought the boat up into the wind for a moment, though there was imminent danger of being swamped, while Kenneth let go the halyards and the mainsail came down with a run. Frank sheeted home the lowered boom, making it solid in its fore and aft position.

Then came the hardest part of all—furling the mainsail. How it was done Kenneth could scarcely tell. He came within an ace of being dashed overboard 20 times, but he escaped at last to reach the cockpit, safe but utterly exhausted. The *Gazelle*, under head sails and jigger only, rode out the gale. Dawn showed the storm-worn boys the entrance to a safe harbor, into which they thankfully crept, and for half the day they slept the deep, dreamless sleep of utter weariness.

Six days later the *Gazelle* sailed into the harbor of Savannah, Kenneth having repaired the gaff in the meantime. She had little of the look of a boat that had passed through a storm that would have been serious for a vessel five times her size. Her crew, however, showed the effects of the battle with the elements; their white working suits were decidedly dingy and the white rubber-soled shoes they wore were sorely in need of pipe clay.

The harbor of Savannah was full of vessels of all sorts and conditions—schooners, two, three and four masters; trim coastwise steamers; and a migratory tramp or two. Kenneth took advantage of the day to examine as closely as possible the lines and construction of the boats in the harbor, and so added to the store of information which he had come so far to glean.

The morning of the *Gazelle*'s departure for waters new, an English tramp churned out of the harbor. As she went past the yacht, Kenneth and Arthur, who were on deck, noticed a man working far aft, coiling down some lines. Suddenly the man dropped his work, leaped the rail and, with arms high in air, jumped into the seething water. Arthur, who was nearest, jumped into *His Nibs*, cast loose the painter, and rowed frantically to the place where he had disappeared, but before he could reach the spot, the man had risen, waved his arms and sunk again. It was hardly a minute before the sailor came up once more, but to the anxious boys it seemed hours. He rose within easy reach of the boat and grasped it with a fervor that dispelled the idea of suicide at once.

Arthur helped him in and rowed him over to the dock, where a burly policeman arrested him for attempted suicide. The rescued man looked out across the harbor and saw his ship steaming off without him, and seemed glad to be within the clutch of the law. The Englishman, for so he proved to be, had been so attracted by the American seaport that he had taken the risk of drowning for the sake of reaching the "land of the brave and the home of the free."

Full of watermelon and in high glee, the young sailors in their trim little ship weighed anchor and sailed down the Savannah River and out on the broad Atlantic on the way to Charleston, South Carolina.

Two days after leaving Savannah the *Gazelle* dropped anchor off Charleston, and for 48 hours the boys went from place to place in the fine harbor, visiting the various points of interest. Fort Sumter, into which the first shot of the Civil War was fired, stood peacefully on its island, deserted, a mere relic of former greatness. The yacht took shelter behind it when a sharp squall came up as she was starting out on her next run northward.

It was the season of squalls, apparently, for they had hardly been 24 hours out from Charleston when Kenneth, observing the mercury of the barometer dropping rapidly, put in to the nearest harbor, Bull Bay, to avoid a stormy night at sea. Instead of a storm, however, the wind fell flat, and for two days the yacht was unable to get out.

The harbor was a beautiful one, but the lack of wind and a blazing sun made life aboard almost unendurable.

"I'd give a farm for an ice cream soda," said Arthur wearily.

Just then Frank came from below. "I heard you fellows say that it was too hot to eat; it's lucky you feel so, for the larder is about empty." Frank had been looking for the wherewithal to get supper.

"You don't mean to say that you haven't anything to eat?" said Kenneth and the mate almost together, their appetites suddenly returning with lamentable strength.

"I've got some beans."

"What's the matter with beans?" Arthur appeared relieved.

A movable oil stove with a makeshift top was rigged on deck in order to give the cabin a chance to cool, and a pot containing the precious beans was set over it to cook.

While the skipper and Frank went ashore to explore, Arthur stayed aboard to keep company with the beans. The two found what Frank declared to be bear tracks, and for some distance they followed them, but the bruin did not show himself. Returning to the yacht, they found Arthur still brooding over the beans, and since there was scarcely anything else to do, the three boys sat under the awning rigged over the main boom and did their best to keep the pot from boiling by persistent watching.

It was getting near seven o'clock, and the boys were already wishing that the beans were done when they saw a little steamboat coming up the bay. She looked familiar, and as she came near all three watched to see if they knew her. At length she drew abeam and they read her name on the paddle-box. A St. Augustine boat on her way to Washington. The yacht and the steamboat had left together, and the yacht had reached Bull Bay two days ahead.

The boat went on her way, and the boys were congratulating

themselves on their good speed, when the swells from the steamboat began to come rolling in. The *Gazelle* commenced to sway.

"The beans!" cried Arthur, and reached for the handle of the pot. Alas, too late! The thing tottered and fell overboard, and Arthur, thinking of nothing but the precious food about to be lost, reached far out after it. A big roller coming in at that precise instant tipped him over, too, and he went head first right into the pot full of beans that had not yet had time to sink.

Arthur rose to the surface the sorriest looking creature that a mere human being could ever manage to be. His hair was plastered with beans, his face framed with them, and the expression on his countenance was woebegone in proportion to the unpleasantness of his predicament. Frank and Kenneth roared with laughter, but Arthur, probably not having the same sense of humor under the circumstances, did not see the joke, and the annoyance on his dismal, bean-plastered face added greatly to their mirth.

Supplies must be procured at once, somehow, somewhere, or the crew would be in danger of starving to death. So the young sailors took advantage of the rising wind to get out of Bull Bay and continue their journey.

The weather conditions were of the best when Kenneth and Arthur turned in, so Frank took the helm alone. The pale gleam of the starlit sky served but to emphasize the darkness, and Frank, steering far out to sea to avoid the long bar of Cape Romain, found it hard to stay awake. It was very late at night, and Arthur and Kenneth were below, sleeping soundly, when they were both awakened by a loud cry from Frank.

Kenneth rushed on deck just as the *Gazelle* rose on the crest of a great breaker.

"Put her about," he shouted. "We're going ashore. Quick!"

Frank put the tiller hard over, and the yacht, responding, spun around, the boom came over swiftly, and, taking Kenneth unaware, knocked him overboard.

"Arthur!" Frank yelled down the companionway. "Come up; Ken's overboard!"

A RACE WITH A GALE

"Ken! Where are you?" Frank's voice was almost drowned by the roaring of the breakers.

It was totally dark, and though both boys strained their eyes to the utmost, not a sign could they see of the skipper, who had vanished in the twinkling of an eye—knocked out of existence, seemingly, but the swinging blow of the boom.

Again they shouted, in unison this time. Surely Kenneth must hear them they thought, if he were still alive and above water.

"Hullo!" The voice was startlingly near. The two looked about quickly in the direction from which the sound came and beheld the skipper hanging on to the end of the boom, far to leeward. His white nightgown was wet and clinging to his long legs, which were waving frantically in the effort to help their owner to crawl along the boom towards the yacht. From time to time as the yawl rolled, the clinging figure was dipped in the sea, and then as suddenly dragged out and swung about like a wet rag on the end of a stick.

For a minute Frank and Arthur stood stupefied. Then, the humor of the situation dawning on them, they began to laugh. This was too much for Kenneth's patience, and he shouted wrathfully, "Trim in that sheet and help me in, will you, you duffers? Do you think I am doing this for your amusement?"

So they hauled in the boom and the dangling captain with it, and landed him safely on deck without a scratch.

With her head turned away from the shoal, the *Gazelle* ran off into deeper water. It was a narrow escape for all hands, but especially so for Ransom, whose quickness in grasping the spar as it swung over had saved his life. Soon he could laugh with the boys over his funny appearance. But he realized, as they could not, by what a narrow margin he had escaped.

After rounding Cape Romain, the *Gazelle* sailed along without mishap of any kind for a day; then the barometer indicated trouble brewing—in fact, the very atmosphere had the feeling of suppressed excitement that almost always precedes a severe storm. Ransom decided that it would be wise to get into a sheltered spot, so he steered for the mouth of Cape Fear River. It was a most difficult place to get into, but once inside, the yacht was perfectly protected from any kind of storm except, perhaps, a cyclone.

No sooner had the anchor been dropped than the wind began to raise its voice from the soft whir-r-r of the summer breeze to the shrill, high shriek of a gale.

"For once," said the skipper, "my foresight was better than my hindsight."

"Good work, old man. I always knew you were a wonder," Frank laughed. "All the same, I'm glad we're inside."

"Mate, put this man in irons. He shall live on bread and water for ten days, due punishment for insubordination and disrespect for a superior officer." Kenneth put on a very grave and judicial air, but could not quite control a twitching of the corners of his mouth, which enlarged to a wide grin when the mate, in obedience to his command, tackled the "crew" and, in the scuffle that followed, went overboard with his "prisoner."

"Never mind the water, mate," Ransom called when the two dripping boys reached the deck. "He has had enough of that, perhaps."

For a week the *Gazelle* lay storm-bound off the little town of Southport on the Cape Fear River. In spite of the rain which fell almost continuously, the boys explored every nook and cranny of the harbor, and pushed up the shallow creeks and examined the sand hills that protected the shipping from the onslaught of the ocean.

The Frying-pan Shoals, extending out into the ocean from the mouth of the Cape Fear River, are responsible for more wrecks than perhaps any other reef on the Atlantic coast. Kenneth got chummy with the pilots who make Southport their headquarters, and they gladly gave him much lore about the channels, beacons, and the ins and outs of the intricate passages all along the coast.

The government required every vessel above a certain tonnage to take on a pilot; or, to be more correct, the vessels were required to pay the pilot's fee whether his services were accepted or not. As the channel was very difficult and the fee had to be paid in any case, the skippers usually turned the responsibility of navigating their vessels into port over to the pilot. The charges were rated according to the ship's depth—the more water she drew, the more difficulty experienced in sailing her over the bars, and the pilot's fee was proportionately large.

One day Kenneth and the mate rowed against the heavy wind a mile and a half to the outer bar, and then went over to the Cape Fear Light. The keeper was inclined to be churlish at first, but as soon as Ransom began to tell him a little about the cruise, his manner changed instantly. Short answers and bored expression gave way to lively interest and voluble requests for more experiences.

"I tell you, Art," Kenneth remarked in an aside to the mate, "a short yarn about the cruise is worth a hundred open-sesames."

The keeper led the two boys up the winding stairs of the lighthouse tower, and as they went round and round, they could hear above the ring of their feet on the iron steps the howling of the wind about the shaft. The power and majesty of it made them pause a minute to listen, and then they felt the shock of the blast, which made even that sturdy tower quiver. When the top was reached and a clear, unobstructed view could be had, the breath of the youngsters was taken away by the awful fury of the elements battling below them. Even the lighthouse keeper was awed by it and kept silent.

From the beach, a little below the foot of the tower, seaward, as far as the eye could reach through the mist and spray, the ocean tossed and rolled. Great hills of water, green and angry, rose as though pushed up from below, their crests lashed into foam and then blown into vapor by the gale. Wave succeeded wave until a mighty host of waters, rank on rank, impelled by the wind, dashed themselves to foam on the ever-resisting shore.

"Oh, this is a fierce place, and no mistake." The honest keeper's words took much of the sublimity out of the scene for the boys. "And a terrible place for wrecks," he continued. "The Frying-pan Shoals run out about 25 miles, and vessels are all the time running afoul of them."

"And in weather like this?" Kenneth inquired.

The keeper made a significant gesture that told, without a word, the horrors of shipwreck, of the despairing efforts of the sailors to work the vessel off the lee shore when the breakers were first seen or heard; of the canvas blown to tatters, the dreadful roar and overpowering rush of the waves driving the vessel on nearer the shoal, staving the boats and washing the crew overboard; and, finally, the sickening jar and shuddering scrape of the ship on the reef. All this the boys saw as the keeper but pointed to the seething waters and the ribs of a wrecked ship showing black against the white foam of the breakers. Many, many places he pointed out to them where good ships rested, never to sail again.

Arthur and Kenneth went back to the yacht with solemn faces and thoughtful minds, very thankful that the Gazelle lay peacefully at anchor, safe.

Though the boys had many pleasant times sailing about the harbor in one of the small boats with which the place was filled—clamming, fishing and swapping stories with the pilots—all hands were glad when the storm abated and they were able to weigh anchor and sail out to sea. The six-sided lighthouse looked very different when the boys saw it the second time. The inlet was little troubled by the heavy rolling seas outside, and reflected the tall, straight shaft of the Cape Fear Light.

The wind had fallen to a strong, steady breeze that kept the Gazelle going at a splendid rate, under all sail reefed once. The sea still showed the effect of the week-long storm. Great, long billows rose and fell, but the yacht coasted gaily over them with many low bows and graceful recoveries.

It was a straightaway sail to Beaufort, North Carolina, and the 120 miles across the broad curve in the land offered, in all its length, not one good harbor.

The wind held true, and gradually the seas flattened out until cruising became a pleasure. Old Ocean seemed bent on making the last sail which the boys would take on its waters as pleasant as possible. The sun sank, and all the skies lit up in honor of his departure; then deep black night succeeded, softly and peacefully, with none of the uncanny feeling of mystery which so ofttimes comes with darkness. The boys felt that the darkness was almost caressing, like a comfortable robe thrown around them, and they looked forward to a long night's sail with a sense of security.

The cabin lamp was lighted, and the mellow glow poured out through the hatch and dead lights; the sailing lights blinked their red and green eyes forward, warning other night prowlers of the sea. Arthur handled the tiller, while Frank and Kenneth lounged easily on either side of the cockpit. Arthur was sailing by compass, for not a sign of land could be seen—all was utterly dark, except where a sea crested near enough to catch the light from one of the lamps.

Steadily the *Gazelle* sailed on, swaying slowly to the swing of the seas, a veritable cradle motion. Kenneth and Frank felt its influence and dozed off; Arthur's duty kept him awake, but all his resolution was required to keep up.

Suddenly, out of the gloom ahead loomed a shape, soft and formless—a huge shadow moving and bearing down on the tiny *Gazelle*.

"Great Scott!" exclaimed Arthur.

"What is it?" Kenneth woke instantly. "Put her over, quick. Hurry."

For the first time since her journeying began, the yacht seemed to hesitate while the great black shadow, which gradually assumed the form of a vessel, bore swiftly down on her. It seemed as if minutes had elapsed before the headsails began to flap and the yawl turned away from her impending doom. Still the great bulk bore down on them silently, without a light showing, the swelling canvas of her sails just indicated by a lighter shade.

"Schooner, ahoy!" Ransom shouted, making a megaphone of his hands. "You're running us down. Bear up, quick!"

A lantern showed high above them on the rail of the schooner, and a woman's shriek rang out, clear and shrill—an uncanny sound to hear at such a time. A creak told of a shifted helm, and the schooner swung to port, clearing the yacht by a few scant inches.

As the vessel slipped by, silent as a shadow, two white faces showed over the rail high above the *Gazelle*. Not a word of excuse did they utter—probably too dazed by the narrow escape to speak.

"Those people ought to be jailed," growled Ransom in his honest indignation. "Sailing without any light."

"Guess they learned their lesson, look!" Sure enough, there was the red gleam of the port light glancing over the waves as it was being fitted into its box.

The next afternoon the *Gazelle* sailed into Beaufort Harbor and the boys bid good-bye to Old Ocean. For a thousand miles they had sailed over its rough waters in all sorts of weathers in a boat scarcely 30 feet long. It was an achievement to be proud of. Not many boys could point to such a record.

"Oh! We are the people!" said Frank, justifiably elated. "It's easy from now on; no more storms, no more breakers, no more broken spars."

"Don't you get a swelled head," the skipper warned. "There is always a pinpoint ready for every bubble."

The *Gazelle* lay at anchor off Beaufort for several days while the boys roamed about the quaint old town. Situated just a little below Cape Hatteras, that terrible storm center, the little city got full benefit of the stormy onshore gales, and there were many signs of the lashings it had received. At one place on Front Street, facing seaward, were some poplar trees whose very name suggests unwavering uprightness, but these were bent in a semi-circle over the houses—a humble acknowledgment of the power of the blast.

The harbor was full of small craft. Boats of every description flitted here and there, like graceful, white-winged dragonflies. Kenneth, for once in his life, saw enough boats, and he got many ideas that he hoped to turn to good account later when he, himself, should become a full-fledged designer.

The night before the *Gazelle* spread her wings to continue her journey, the three boys were lying about on deck after supper enjoying the evening breeze. It was just about dusk, and sky and water were assuming their most beautiful opalescent tints. It was a time to encourage sentiment, and each of the boys felt a trifle of pleasant sadness as they thought of their far-off homes and the loved ones there. Off in the distance some people were singing a familiar college air.

It was all so like some of the evenings the boys had spent off old St. Joe that the unfamiliar things about them changed their shapes and positions until they almost dreamed that they were indeed at home. The voices came nearer, and a trim white yacht carrying the singers rose out of the dusk and sped swiftly towards them. When the two boats were within a hundred yards of each other, the singers changed their tune to *Michigan, My Michigan*.

This completed the spell, and for the first time the captain and crew had a genuine case of homesickness. Neither of the three dared to look the other in the face.

"*Gazelle*, ahoy!"

The hail rang clear and sharp over the smooth water, and its suddenness woke the boys from their daydreams instantly. It was long since they had heard that hail.

"Aye—who goes there?" was the answer.

"A friend!"

"Approach, friend, and let us look at you."

The yacht swooped around the *Gazelle*'s stern and headed up into the wind, her sails flapping. She dropped her anchor and soon the yawl's deck and cabin were filled with gay visitors. One of them knew some of Kenneth's people, which acquaintance both visitors and visited considered quite sufficient.

The boys hated to weigh anchor next morning and leave the pleasant place and the friends they had just made, but the thought of the thousands of miles yet to be traversed urged them on.

"And just think of leaving those watermelons at two cents each!" The sadness in Arthur's voice told of his sincere regret.

The first day's sail brought the voyagers to the end of Core Sound. They were just below Hatteras and inside, but it looked as if the stormy old cape was not going to allow them to pass without giving them an experience to remember him by. The wind was rising rapidly and the massing of the heavy clouds cast a shadow over all.

"We're in for another blow, I guess," said the skipper as he pulled on his sticky oilskins. "This old boat is getting tried out pretty well."

As the *Gazelle* flew past the Royal Shoal light, the keeper and his family waving good luck, the gale was blowing its best out of the east and, close-hauled, the yacht flew along in a smother of foam, her lee rail awash, her sails as hard as if of molded tin, her rigging taut and humming like harp strings.

Just before she reached Gull Shoal light, her gaff snapped again and, with reduced canvas, she hurried along. Frank and Arthur lay forward to look for channel marks and for whatever troubles might chance, while Kenneth steered. The heavy clouds shut down on them like night. The darkness seemed thick enough to cut, and not a thing could be seen but the white-capped waves that dashed madly by them. They were like a man who, being pursued, runs at full speed through a perfectly dark passage that is not familiar to him—he must run on, yet he knows not at what moment he may dash himself against a wall or trip and fall headlong.

It was a time of breathless excitement and constant, unnerving fear, lest the yacht, flying along at almost railroad speed, should run into one of the numerous shoals that lay spread like a net for the unwary, and dash herself to pieces.

The heavy rain obliterated every sign of a channel mark, and the thick storm clouds shut off the sun as completely as a total eclipse. Kenneth had to steer by compass only.

Frank and Arthur peered ahead, their hands raised to shield their eyes from the driving rain. A long shoal ran out into the sound, and all hands were trying to make out the lighthouse that marked it.

Ransom thought it the hardest blow he had ever known, and he wondered how long the sturdy little craft he sailed could stand the strain. The wind tugged at the canvas, tried all the stays, but beyond the makeshift gaff, apparently, could find nothing vulnerable.

It seemed as if the squall lasted hours, but when the rain finally stopped and the wind lessened in force, the boys saw the dim outlines of the lighthouse off the port bow, and they knew it could not have lasted much over two hours. As they passed the light, the keeper rang his bell in salute and shouted his congratulations.

"It's the worst short storm I've seen in many years," he shouted. "You're lucky to get through safely."

When the mate went below to put on some dry clothes, he looked at the tin clock and discovered that the *Gazelle* had covered the distance between the two lights—16 miles—in about an hour and a quarter.

At Stumpy Bay they stopped to make a new gaff, and after a two-day layoff there, they went on to Coin Jock, North Carolina.

A fleet of barges loaded with watermelons, going through the canal leading through the Dismal Swamp to Norfolk, offered to give the boys a tow—an invitation which they hastened to accept. Not until nine o'clock did the procession start, with the *Gazelle* at the end of the long line of boats. It was a dark, lowering night, and not a thing could the boys see of the country through which they were passing. The light of the boat ahead was their only guide.

The yacht was snapped to and fro on the end of the long line of boats like the end boy on a Snap-the-Whip string. About midnight the rain began to come down in a perfect deluge, and the word was passed aft to each boat to anchor until things cleared.

Though the boys could see little but the jagged outlines of the trees against the stormy sky, they voted the surroundings dismal enough to merit the name.

Just before daylight the fleet got underway again, the little *Gazelle* tagging on behind like a reluctant boy hanging on to his mother's hand when she takes him shopping.

At Norfolk Ransom and his shipmates found a goodly company of vessels of all sorts, all rigs, and every nationality. The red-and-black storm flag was flying from every signal station along the coast, and the vessels had hastened to cover in Hampton Roads and Norfolk harbor.

Returning from the post office, where Kenneth and the mate found a goodly batch of precious home letters awaiting them, they had great difficulty in making headway against the gale that was already blowing. The anchorage reached, they realized anew how cozy and comfortable the *Gazelle*'s cabin was.

"Let's have a watermelon in honor of... well... to celebrate this occasion." It was Arthur, of course, who suggested this.

"In honor of what occasion?" Frank winked at the skipper.

"The watermelon and the fellows who gave it to us."

So each boy, a section of the pink fruit in one hand and a letter in the other, began the absorbing process of eating and reading.

The wind was playing high jinx outside, but the young tars in their snug cabin heeded it not a bit. Not until a stream of pink melon juice squirted over the written page which he was reading did Kenneth look up, his attention distracted. The darkness of the cabin made him look for the cause.

To port, flashes of the gray, stormy light were sifting in through the oval windows when the yacht rose to the top of a wave; then he turned to the right and looked out. A great black wall shut off every particle of light—it was as if the yacht had been built against a high board fence.

Kenneth jumped out and ran on deck.

"Look out, boys!" he shouted down the hatch after a moment. "The big schooner just to starboard of us is dragging her anchors and will be down on us in a minute."

CAPTURED BY "LIBERTY"

When Arthur and Frank came on deck in answer to Kenneth's summons, the wind nearly took their heads off—it blew in their ears and deafened them. They found it hard to breathe against it and its force nearly took them off their pins.

"What's the trouble, old ma——?"

Frank stopped in the middle of the word as he caught sight of the black bulk of the schooner slowly bearing down upon them. Scarcely 20 feet of worried and wind-swept water separated the two vessels.

Nearer and nearer she came until, to the excited eyes of the crew, it seemed as if the big boat would swallow the smaller one whole.

The mate went forward, a big clasp knife in hand to cut the cable, if that extreme move became necessary.

Kenneth had shouted to the captain of the schooner at the outset, and all hands were trying everything to stop her backward progress. There was no time to raise sails and beat out of the danger, and it certainly looked as if the *Gazelle* would be crushed like an eggshell, or else cut adrift to run the very probable chances of being dashed against the spiles of the piers.

It was a strange situation. In the harbor, between the two populous cities of Norfolk and Portsmouth, in the midst of a large fleet of seaworthy boats humming with life, one great bully of a vessel was slowly closing down on a smaller one. Tens of thousands of people almost within call, yet none could stir hand or foot to help. Nor could the crew of either craft do aught to prevent imminent peril.

The *Gazelle* tugged at her moorings as if she realized the danger and longed eagerly to be free. The crew of the schooner hung over the rail aft, watching the narrowing strip of water.

The suspense was tremendous, and each boy showed the effects of it according to his temperament. Kenneth stood with tightly shut fists and clenched jaws, but otherwise showed no signs of the anxiety he felt. Frank could not keep still but twitched, rose and sat down again a hundred times while the rain ran down the locks of long black hair over his face unheeded. Arthur, who was forward, ready to cut the cables if necessary, was possessed with the desire to do something; he found it hard to wait and appealed to Kenneth many times to know if he should sever the anchor line.

The movement of the large ship was so gradual that it seemed as if the moment of contact would never arrive. If the end would only come quickly, or if they could but do something to end the suspense! Anything would be a relief. They watched with staring eyes the slow approach of the larger vessel—so slow that the movement was scarcely perceptible.

Suddenly Frank spoke in the startled tone of one who wakes from a nightmare. "She isn't moving! The anchor must have caught at last." The three tried to measure the distance between the boats to see if Frank's assertion was really true.

"You are right, old man," Kenneth said at last. "Luck is with us again."

It was a mighty narrow escape—the space between the two boats could almost be covered by an active jumper.

Later in the day the schooner that had threatened to crush the yacht was the means by which she was saved from another danger.

It was growing dark when the captain of the schooner hailed the *Gazelle* and told Kenneth that he wanted to shift his anchorage. The wind was still blowing a gale, and the waves slapped viciously at everything that withstood them.

The *Gazelle* was holding fast to the bottom with two anchors, but when the boys tried to raise the largest it stuck and could not be moved, so the end of the cable was buoyed and let go. Immediately the yacht began to drag the anchor that remained, as if it were but a heavy stone, and drifted swiftly toward the bulkheads of the wharfs. Again the possibility of a smash-up confronted them.

"On board the schooner!" Kenneth shouted against the wind in the direction of the larger craft. But the wind carried the words back to him mockingly. Again he shouted: "We're dragging anchor. Throw us a line! Throw us a line!"

It seemed ages before anyone appeared. Then the face of the captain showed itself. He immediately grasped the situation and in the nick of time threw a long line to them. Arthur caught it and made it fast, while the captain did likewise on the schooner. Once more the *Gazelle* was saved; she swung on the end of the long rope like the cork on a fishing line.

For a week the storm continued; so for many days the captain and crew of the yacht had nothing to do but go sightseeing, write letters and play games. Whenever the weather permitted, *His Nibs* was brought alongside and one or two of the boys went ashore.

On one side of the narrow harbor was Norfolk, one of the big and growing cities of the south. Her docks were filled with ocean-going and coast-wise craft, steamers and sailing vessels of every rig. Situated on a fine harbor, a point from which railroads radiated within easy reach of the coal fields and iron mines, and but a short distance from the great shipbuilding yards at Newport News, it prospered exceedingly. There was little about it that suggested the southern city, except the multitude of colored people who roamed the streets.

Across the stream-like harbor lay Portsmouth, a much smaller place, on a lower scale of development. In its navy yard many of the ships that did such good service during the war with Spain were fitted out. Then its shops were kept going day and night; the workmen swarmed like bees in and out of the buildings, and the place resounded with the loud, gong-like ring of blows on cavernous boilers and the sharp tap-tap of the riveters. It was quite different when the boys visited it: Many of the shops were closed and the marines, clad from head to foot in rubber, who paced to and fro in front of the old stone buildings, had little to do, for there were few frolicsome jackies to make trouble for them.

Kenneth, Arthur and Frank visited the shipping, the oyster markets, where hundreds of the trim oyster sloops and schooners were unladen weekly, the navy yard, St. Paul's, the old stone church built in 1739 which still bore high in its tower the round shot fired into it during the War of 1812, and last, but far from least, the watermelon fleet.

"How's business?" they inquired interestedly.

"Rotten," was the reply, and the truth of it was evident in the piles of discarded fruit about. Great, luscious melons were selling at $3.50 per hundred, and buyers were hard to find at that. Whether the boys went singly or by twos, they always returned laden to their utmost capacity with the great, green fruit.

The tenth day after their arrival in Norfolk, Kenneth got up early and, in a voice fit to wake the dead, roared: "Up, all hands. Break yourselves out of your bunks, there. This is the day we 'move de boat'; up, all hands!"

The other two got up, yawning and stretching, to find the sun streaming warmly through the lights. Breakfast was cooked and eaten, dishes washed and put away, decks scrubbed, brass rubbed and rigging examined. The bugler aboard the U.S.S. *Texas*, anchored but a short distance off, was just blowing reveille when the boys began to heave on the anchor cable. But it was long after the shrill boatswain's call to mess had sounded aboard the *Texas* before the *Gazelle's* crew gave up the task of hauling aboard the anchor.

The boys hauled and tugged until it seemed as if the bow of the *Gazelle* would be pulled down to keep company with the anchor, but not an inch would it budge. It was provoking that, when wind and tide favored and pleasant weather promised, they should be held to land.

Kenneth stood with frowning brows looking along the straight cable while the perspiration stood in beads on his face, gazing as if he would pierce the green-brown flood with his glance and see what held the mudhook fast. Arthur and Frank stood by silent and hot, for the sun beat down fiercely. All three were dry of suggestions, for everything had been tried.

"Oh, let's try once more; then if the pesky thing won't come up we'll cut adrift and leave it." Kenneth was at the end of his patience.

Once more the windlass was set going, and with the aid of three pairs of strong, young arms the heavy manila line was stretched taut until the yacht's bow was pulled a foot or more below the normal water line, but not an inch would the old anchor budge. But just as the boys were on the verge of giving up in desperation, the rollers from a passing tug tossed the yacht and gave an extra heavy pull on the line. Suddenly the yawl regained her level and inch by inch the refractory anchor was yanked up. A great, water-soaked log clinging to one of the flukes revealed the cause of the trouble when it reached the surface.

Free at last from the grasp of the land, the *Gazelle* threaded her way past trim, converted yacht-gunboats (which looked little like the venomous terriers of war they were), the grim *Texas*, whose peaceful white coating of paint belied her destructive, death-dealing power, and past the battered *Reina Mercedes*, which, in spite of every effort of her former owner, was destined to become a useful member of Uncle Sam's navy.

Indeed, yachts, steamers, steamboats and sailing craft of every description were passed by the *Gazelle* on her way to the open bay, the famous Hampton Roads. Many hands were waved in salute to the little craft and her sturdy crew, and no less numerous were the toots of the whistles which greeted them, for the fame of their trip had spread until the little white yawl was almost as well known to the shipping population as the members of the white squadron.

When the sun of August 22nd sent its last rays over the beautiful Hampton Roads, the *Gazelle* had rounded Old Point Comfort and left the picturesque old Fortress Monroe astern. Long after sundown the *Gazelle* wended her way up the broad Chesapeake Bay, one of a thousand craft that sped over its smooth waters.

Soon the moon rose in perfect splendor, and as the boys sat in the cockpit, spellbound by the beauty of the scene, they saw a great Baltimore clipper, square-rigged, every sail spread, come sailing down the broad path of moonlight. Leaning a trifle to the strength of the breeze, every sail rounded out and bathed in silvery light, her keen prow turning the phosphorescent waves like a plow-share, she made one of the finest pictures mortal man ever beheld. The sight made the boys' sailor-blood stir within them, and they stood spellbound until the great ship swept majestically by, silent but for the splash of the waves as she spurned them aside, or the creak of a block under the strain of swelling canvas.

The yacht held her course until long after midnight, sailing by the light of the moon. Then she dropped anchor in one of the innumerable indentations that mark the coastline of the bay.

It was late the next morning when the three young mariners rubbed their eyes open, but they might as well have turned in again, for hardly a breath of wind was stirring and the swift tide was running out—downstream. For three days the wind failed them. Then a breeze sprang up that made the resisting tide of no avail.

The *Gazelle* sailed along past sandy beaches and rocky points, past fascinating marshy nooks and bluff headlands, at what seemed a good round gait until a slim, rakish-looking craft went by so quickly that the yacht might just as well have been anchored, so great was the contrast in speed.

"Well, I'll be switched," was Kenneth's surprised exclamation. Never had he seen his boat left behind so quickly before. "Bet she's got a gasoline engine stowed aft there somewhere."

"No, the *Gazelle* is foul with weeds and things."

"We'll have to lay her up and scrape her, then," was Kenneth's determined reply. He could not have his craft beaten like that, without a protest.

The cause of all this dissatisfaction flew by like the shadow of a swiftly moving cloud. Her masts were raked sharply aft, and her two enormous leg-o'-mutton sails were out of all proportion to her beam, the boys thought. The hull was built of five or six large logs, hollowed out and cleverly joined with peculiarly shaped wooden pegs that held the connecting logs closely together. It was a new sort of craft to Ransom, and his respect for the Chesapeake Bay fishermen increased as he realized the careful seamanship required to keep a "Bugeye" right-side up.

Past the mouth of the Potomac River, which led directly to the national capital, sailed the three boys, though they longed with all their might for a sight of Washington, and it took all their resolution to keep headed up the bay. Old Annapolis, the seat of the naval academy and the place where so many naval heroes had been educated, was left without a visit, but each boy promised himself that he would return and see everything sometime. The names Dewey, Sampson, Schley, Evans, Philip, Hobson and a host of others were on everybody's tongue at that time, and yet the three young mariners (so pressed for time were they) could not visit the place where these great men had been educated.

Just before reaching Chesapeake City the yacht was beached and when the tide receded, the boys found barnacles and sea moss to the thickness of three-fourths of an inch or more on its bottom. The planking beneath, however, was as sound as could be and showed not a sign of the many terrific strains to which it had been subjected.

At Chesapeake City the yacht entered the Chesapeake and Delaware Canal, the Haul Over Canal, as it is generally called. Kenneth was told that he would have to pay $11 for the privilege of passing through the lock and for the hire of five mules to tow the yawl through.

"But I don't want a tow through," he protested.

"But yer got ter." The driver was very emphatic. "The law says yer got ter take a tow troo."

"The *Gazelle* is light; one mule would be enough, and you have five."

"Yer gotter have five. But we'll snake yer throo quick." This last was said with the air of one who is conferring a great favor.

"The first time I ever drove five-in-hand," said Arthur, laughing, as the driver whipped up and the yacht began tearing through the water. It was a pleasant ride through that short canal. The mules kept on at a steady trot, and the trees and an occasional house went flying past. At six o'clock the lock opening into the Delaware River at Delaware City was reached but, as the tide was wrong, the *Gazelle* did not float into the historic stream until several hours later.

The river was full of moving craft when the *Gazelle* swung into the stream. Great ocean-going steamers, disreputable looking tramp steamships, trim schooners of every size, and here and there a yacht. The scene was full of animation and color, busy boats and busy people—very different from the easygoing life which the boys had just left on the southern water courses.

Towns with factories whose smoking chimneys told of active work dotted the river bank every mile or two, and in between were fields of flourishing crops. Not a foot of ground was wasted.

Headwinds delayed the little craft much, and the smoky haze that hung over the great city of Philadelphia was not sighted until the fourth day after leaving Delaware City.

"We're just in time. Look!" Frank pointed through the rain-like fog that greeted the young voyagers on their first visit to the City of Brotherly Love.

"What— Say, that's fine!"

It was an exclamation that the sight before them extracted involuntarily. Anchored in two long lines lay a fleet of Uncle Sam's dogs of war. Painted white, they looked like great ghosts of ships through the fog; all was gray except where the beautiful red, white and blue showed dimly through, or where the red, yellow and blue signal flags on the flagship made spots of color in the general dullness. In and about darted the man-o-war launches like the restless, ever-moving insects which one sees on placid pools in summer.

The procession was Philadelphia's tribute to the victorious hosts in the war with Spain, and the boys came in just the nick of time to take in all the goings on—the parades of soldiers and sailors and the still more interesting, ever-restless procession of the multitude of people from every direction.

Everything was open, from the United States Mint and Independence Hall, where Congress first met, to Cramp's shipyard and the University of Pennsylvania buildings. During the three days our mariners lay off the city, they saw it all. Kenneth would have been at Cramp's shipyard to this day if Arthur had not pulled him off by main force. The great enclosure from which so many of America's famous ships had been launched had a strong fascination for him, and it was only with the greatest difficulty that he tore himself away.

Underway once more, the *Gazelle* soon reached Bordentown where she entered the Delaware and Raritan Canal. Surprised and delighted at the small canal fee, Kenneth paid the $2.80 and, with a long line, he and Arthur began to tow to Trenton (six miles). As luck would have it, Kenneth and his friends met the owner of the steam yacht *Cora* at Trenton, who was also going through the canal.

The story of the trip thus far and the plans for the remainder of the journey so interested the *Cora*'s master that he wanted to hear more of it and offered to tow the *Gazelle* through for the sake of the society of her captain and crew. The boys thought this more than a fair exchange and accepted with pleasure. The *Gazelle* seemed to feel the importance of her position and strutted behind the graceful *Cora* as though she were merely following the larger and more fashionable vessel, and was not submitting to anything so undignified as towing.

"The old boat will get so stuck up with her five-mule team and now her steam-yacht tow, that she'll outgrow her headsails."

"Wait 'til she strikes the Erie Canal, when her fall cometh. It's lucky if we get even one horse to tow her then."

Along the broad canal the two yachts went at a pace that the boys thought too fast, for little opportunity was given to them to see the many interesting things that they passed so quickly.

At New Brunswick, the end of the canal, the *Gazelle*'s crew bid their kind friends good-bye and, hoisting sail, went on alone. As they drew nearer and nearer the metropolis—the city which they had heard about all their lives but never seen and which, next to their own homes, was the place of all others that they desired to reach—their nerves tingled with excitement, and the good, round pace which the *Gazelle* was making seemed all too slow.

When darkness fell they were but seven miles below New Brunswick, on the Raritan River, anchored in a spot that seemed absolutely remote from civilization, above all far from a great city, so quiet was it. Undisturbed by sight of anyone, the three youngsters made the night hideous with their jubilant songs, bawled at the tops of their voices. Well might they be joyful, for surely the thing accomplished more than justified their exultation.

In a 30-foot boat they had braved the treacherous Gulf and the savage Atlantic, travelled dangerous waters without a pilot. These mere boys who had never seen salt water before this cruise, with barely enough money to pay the narrowest expenses and buy the cheapest possible food, were now within a day's sail of New York, sound and well, with a boat under them that was as fit as when she had slipped into the fresh waters of far-off Lake Michigan.

"Hip, hip! Hurrah!" they shouted over the placid waters of the Raritan River; and well they might.

Next day Kenneth steered his craft past Perth Amboy into the Arthur Kills back of Staten Island, and that evening saw them anchored off Elizabethport. Pretty much the same sort of feeling that rouses a child on Christmas morning at daybreak brought Kenneth, Arthur and Frank on deck before the sun had fairly started his day's work. It was September 7th and the red and black sweaters with the word "*Gazelle*" embroidered on the breast were found very comfortable in the chill morning air. A haze hung over everything, and the boats that were moving slipped about as if on tiptoe, fearful lest the sleeping millions be awakened too soon.

As the *Gazelle* rounded Bergen Point, Jersey City, and sailed into the Upper New York Bay, boats seemed to spring out of the very water—ferry boats, sailboats, tugs. Never had the boys seen so many craft in motion before.

A haze still hung over the water, and objects only 200 yards off could be seen but dimly.

"There's the Statue of Liberty," Arthur cried excitedly.

Sure enough, the great statue stood before them—her torch held on high, the heavy vapor wreathed about her like beautiful, filmy drapery.

Putting helm to starboard, the *Gazelle* turned to go inside Bedloe's Island.

"Look, can't you see a tall building over there?" All the boys looked for the jagged skyline which they had seen pictured so often, and soon became so intent that they forgot to watch where they were going.

With a sudden bump and a sickening jar, the *Gazelle* stopped short. She was hard and fast on the cruel rocks.

FROM NEW YORK TO ALBANY

With the very shadow of the great Liberty statue stretching over them, their good ship was fast on the rocks and threatening to spring a leak any moment. Shipwreck at the gates of America's greatest city stared the boys in the face. They had encountered sandbars, ice, great waves and fierce winds, but not until New York Harbor received them so inhospitably had the *Gazelle*'s keel struck rock.

Quick work was necessary if the yacht were to be saved, for even now the rollers from passing steamboats were causing her to pound.

Without a word, Kenneth jumped forward, lowered jib and mainsail and then, without stopping to take off any clothes, sprang overboard.

"Come on, boys!" he cried. In another instant all three were lifting and pushing the heavy hull to get her off the rocks into the deep water of the channel, straining with all their might. Hot work it was, despite the cool water that wet them. Reluctantly the yacht began to slide backward. Lifted by the rollers and pushed by three sturdy backs, she slipped towards the channel until the boys found themselves without a footing and hanging on the boat for support. She was afloat once more.

"Thank God!" said Ransom fervently, as he climbed on deck, dripping and shivering in the chill morning air. Once more the good ship had withstood the test.

A few minutes were spent in putting on dry clothes, then on up New York Bay they went. All was plain sailing until the yacht's straight bowsprit poked itself around old Fort William Henry on Governor's Island. Then the fun began.

The two great currents from the North and East Rivers met off the fort, each carrying an immense number of craft of all sorts going in every direction. Whistles tooted, bells clanged, and paddlewheels and churning propellers turned the green waters into frothing chaos.

Kenneth and his friends were bewildered, and they wondered how they were ever going to pilot the diminutive *Gazelle* through that intricate labyrinth of shifting vessels.

The monster *Kaiser Wilhelm der Grosse*, her huge hull dragged by several tugs (reminding one of a large piece of bread being moved off by ants), blocked the way to starboard, while one of the swift Sandy Hook boats dashed by to port, leaving a great wave astern. The Long Island Sound boats, veritable floating hotels, were just rounding the battery on the way to their piers ahead, and to and fro the tugboats puffed on erratic courses. Shuttles they were, that seemed to be weaving a net from which the yacht could not escape.

"Phew!" whistled Kenneth, who was steering. "How the deuce are we going to get through this, I would like to know!"

"I don't see, unless we sink and go underneath." Arthur's brows were puckered with perplexity, curious to see, but perfectly simple to understand.

"I don't know how, but we always do get out of our scrapes somehow. Still,—well, will you look at that, in the name of common sense!" Frank stopped from sheer astonishment.

The yacht was speeding down a narrow lane between two great outgoing ships, a great schooner and an English tramp, her way clear for once, when a tug appeared across the opening. At the end of a long towline a half-dozen canal boats strung out—a barrier 600 yards long, at least. Kenneth trimmed in his sheets quickly, put his helm to starboard and started to go around the end of the tow, but no sooner had the yacht gathered headway in the new direction than a big ferryboat ran from behind the tramp, and she had to luff quickly to avoid a collision.

"This is getting tiresome, to say the least," remarked Kenneth in a vexed tone. "I guess we'll have to follow Arthur's suggestion and make a submarine trip of it."

"Look at that sloop, there—she goes right along and the steam craft get out of her way." Arthur pointed out a well-loaded oyster boat. "If we only had our nerve with us, we'd be all right."

"It takes nerve, but here goes. We have the right of way."

Sure enough, whenever there seemed to be no escape from an accident and the yacht pluckily pushed on, the steam vessels shifted to one side ever so slightly and allowed her to pass.

At first the excitement was too great for comfort, but as they proceeded up the river unharmed, it began to be exhilarating. Great ferryboats crossed their bows so near that they could almost jump aboard. Tugs steamed by so close that the crews of the two boats easily passed the time of day in an ordinary tone of voice. Huge steamers passed that might have stowed the *Gazelle* on one of their decks without inconveniencing their promenading passengers in the slightest.

"And yet," said Frank, bending his head far back in order to see a steamer's rail, "this little boat weathered some storms that would make even that vast hull tremble." He voiced the thought that all of them had in mind.

With eyes bright with interest, the boys saw the graceful sweep of the Brooklyn Bridge, the tall, red, square tower of the Produce Exchange, and the brownstone spire of historic Trinity Church set in the midst of, and almost dwarfed by, the higher buildings about it. Towering 10, 20 or 30 stories high, the great office buildings made a skyline strangely jagged and bold. As the yacht sailed northward, the city flattened out somewhat, and the moving network made by the wakes of the shifting boats became more open.

Off 72nd Street, at the beginning of Riverside Drive, the anchor was dropped and, now out of the stream of passing craft, the crew stopped to take a quiet breath and recover from the excitement of navigating a great waterway full of swiftly moving vessels of every nationality going to and from every part of the world.

A week of sightseeing followed. Now, perhaps for the first

time, the boys longed for money with a longing born not out of need, but at the sight of the many attractive things that can be bought for small sums, and the interesting shows which their empty pockets did not permit them to enjoy. Of the free shows, hardly a one escaped them: the museums of art and natural history, the New York Zoo in Bronx Park and the great buildings and public parks all received their share of attention. Though comparisons may be odious, the boys put the Natural History and Metropolitan Art museums beside the Field Columbian Museum in Chicago, and discussed hotly among themselves the relative merits of each.

His Nibs was a hard-worked boat those days, because from four to six times a day it ferried the boys to and from the yacht. Perhaps it was because it was tired of so much work that it floated itself into the attention of a couple of young "wharf rats" one evening.

Kenneth had come ashore alone and made the small boat fast to the landing close to the shore end of a long, closely built wharf. For perhaps three hours he was away, and when he returned it was after 11 o'clock and black night. Reaching the landing, he found the boat missing, and his heart sank, for he had an affection for the little craft that had done its work so bravely; besides, he could ill afford the money to replace it.

Suddenly he awoke to the fact that just beyond his sight, a boat was being rowed hurriedly away. Running down the stringpiece to the end of the pier, he saw two young reprobates paddling off with all their might in *His Nibs*. What should he do? Not a policeman in sight, not a boat in which he could follow near at hand. He feared he would have to let his boat be taken before his very eyes. But all at once a thought struck him and the humor of it made him smile as he started to put it into operation. With a big clasp knife he carried in his pocket he thought that he might bluff the thieves into thinking that it was a revolver and so scare them into returning the stolen property.

Running out to the end of the pier where his figure would be silhouetted against the distant light, he pulled out his knife and, holding it as if it were a revolver, pointed it at the wharf rats.

"Where are you going with that boat?" he shouted in stern

tones.

No answer, though the thieves stopped rowing.

"You return that boat or I'll—" Kenneth left his sentence unfinished, but he flourished his impromptu revolver so fiercely that the boat stealers were evidently cowed.

"Get that boat back, and be quick about it. No fooling, or I'll shoot you full of holes." Kenneth could hardly keep his face straight when he saw them back water and turn to go back to the landing. "I was just in time," he said to himself, as he followed along on the stringpiece. "If they ever got under a dock, it would be all day with *His Nibs*."

Arriving at the float, the boys (who were hardly out of their teens, Kenneth thought) started for the street on a run. Ransom stayed not for pursuit, but jumped into the boat and pushed off. Once the two stopped to look back, but a threatening move with the knife sent them on with renewed speed.

"Well, that's the best joke," Kenneth said to himself, and he stopped rowing to pat the pocket where he had dropped the knife.

September 14th broke bright and clear, with a touch of the keen autumnal vigor in the air. A good, strong breeze was blowing, and the boys weighed anchor with light hearts, for they were beginning the last 1500 miles of their 7000-mile journey. On up the Hudson River the good yacht sped, the smooth green lawns of Riverside Park on one side, the frowning cliffs of Jersey Heights on the other. Soon the dome of Grant's Tomb was passed, dazzling white and gleaming in the morning sun.

Hour after hour the little boat sailed up the majestic stream, a mere moving mote on the broad, watery ribbon. To the east, the land sloped gently to the stream, an undulating green country dotted here and there with towns and clumps of factory buildings. On the western shore, the giant Palisades stood bluff and impressive, a solid stone wall from 200 to 500 feet high and 15 miles long.

The boys speedily became mere animated exclamation points, for hardly a minute passed that did not disclose some new beauty, some unexpected vista.

The breeze held fair all day and, the night being clear, the young navigators sailed on until long after sundown. The close attention and long day's sail made captain and crew so tired that, when they turned in rather late, they slept like logs.

At seven o'clock the next morning, all aboard were as thoroughly at home in the land of Nod as if they intended to spend the rest of their days there. Old Sol was shining brightly over the eastern hills; the summer breeze had not gained its full strength and made but a ripple on the smooth surface of the river. It was a quiet, peaceful scene that had not a suggestion of noise or turmoil of any kind.

Of a sudden there was a tremendous report, an explosion that rent the air. Then, in quick succession, like a veritable bombardment, numerous detonations followed.

The first blast fairly shook the boys out of their snug bunks, and they tumbled out on deck wide-eyed, fearing they knew not what. The air was filled with a tremendous roar that echoed and re-echoed across from one height to another.

"Good heavens!" Frank exclaimed when he turned to the west. "We're done, sure."

The whole side of the cliff seemed to be coming down on them. Blast after blast went off, each louder than the preceding one, and with each report the earth shook and fountains of dust, smoke and bits of rock flew up.

All three boys stood dazed, amazed, almost unnerved, indeed, until they realized that the rock was being blasted out of the cliff for paving purposes.

"That's a nice way to wake a fellow up," said Arthur in a tone of supreme disgust, when the last charge had been fired and the smoke had in part cleared away.

"I guess that's about the only thing that would have waked us, though," said Kenneth, yawning. "Will you look at that scar in the face of the cliff? That's what I call a blooming shame." A great, broad, red-brown scar on the abrupt rise showed bare beside the green and gray rocks on either side.

Suddenly Frank burst out into a laugh and ran quickly below. "Look at that big boat full of people coming down the river, and then get below. You're unfit for publication."

Kenneth and Arthur looked as they were bidden, then suddenly realized that they were all still clad in their abbreviated night clothes. Instantly, all that could be seen of the three lads was their entirely respectable heads, and when the steamboat went by, these three nodded a greeting and three arms, browned by the sun, waved in salute.

The next morning found the yawl at Poughkeepsie. Behind them were the mountains that have guarded the stream for centuries, Storm King, old Dunderberg and the lesser heights. West Point, with the fine buildings of the U.S. military academy crowning its high plateau, lay below them. Anchored almost in the shadow of the great Poughkeepsie Bridge, one of the most wonderful structures in the world, the boys thought they were certainly getting their money's worth in the sightseeing line.

Their tongues kept up a continual clatter until long after dark.

"Did you ever see anything like that view at West Point?"

"Wasn't that a dandy, big steamboat that passed us near Newburgh?"

"I tell you that big mountain near Peekskill was great. Made a fellow feel like two for a nickel."

And so the talk went on, until finally tired nature overcame even the excitement of novel experiences, and they fell asleep.

The 76 miles to Albany was covered the next day, in spite of the adverse current; by nightfall the *Gazelle* was anchored almost within sight of the Empire State's Capitol building.

The first thing Kenneth did at Albany the next morning was to apply to the state superintendent of public works, Colonel Partridge, for a permit to go through the Erie Canal—the long link in the chain that was to carry the cruisers to their native lakes again. Colonel Partridge was so cordially interested in the cruise that he introduced Kenneth and his friends to some newspaper men. So for the time they were the talk of the town.*

With his permit in his pocket, Kenneth went uptown to see a friend of his father's, who was holding some money for him that he needed very badly. As usual, the story of the cruise had to be told at length and with much detail, and it was late when the captain finally took his departure, at peace with all the world by reason of the roll of greenbacks in his pocket, and of the good

---

* The writer is indebted to Colonel Partridge for the first information about the cruise and the cruisers, and he takes pleasure in acknowledging his obligation.

things in the inner boy. Clad in his navy blue sailor blouse, he walked with the true sailor swing down to the riverfront, and putting his fingers to his lips blew the shrill signal to his shipmates to notify them that he was ready to go aboard. It was a long way to the yacht, and Kenneth, putting his back to a spile, prepared to take it easy while he waited for the small boat.

Like most great cities, the dives, the cut-throat saloons and places of that sort were situated near the waterfront, spread like a spider's web for the unwary sailor. Ransom noticed as he walked through the narrow streets towards the river that the saloons were disgorging their disreputable patrons prior to closing up, and several times he had crossed to the other side to avoid direct contact with them.

The arc lights along the street cast a flare of strong light directly about the poles supporting them, but a little way off the shadows were correspondingly dense. Lurking in one of these spots of shadow, Kenneth saw the figure of a man approaching him noiselessly. There was that about him which told that he had been drinking.

A stray ray of light showed the boy the cruel, debased face, and he looked about for a way of escape. The buildings fronting on the street were closed tight, their inhabitants fast asleep—no shelter there; back of him the river lay black, ready to completely engulf whatever might fall into it. "And I haven't got a thing to defend myself with," the boy said to himself. The drunken man approached nearer, an unpleasant leer on his face.

"Say, Jack, give us the price of a drink," he said in a tone that suggested more clearly than words, "or it will be the worse for you."

Kenneth thought of the roll of bills in his pocket and glanced at the dark water below him. Then, like a flash, it occurred to him that the bum had taken him for a sailor—a man-o'-warsman—and a plan suggested itself to him which he immediately proceeded to put into execution.

It was rather difficult for him to assume the gruff, husky voice of a hard drinker, but he managed it pretty well. "Sorry I can't 'commodate you, mate," he said, gruffly, "but I'm busted—clean, and looking for a berth. Got shore leave and blew all my dough.

Got jagged and don't know how to get back to the ship."

The boy almost gagged at the language, but he played the game well and the bluff worked, for the drunk was satisfied. He said something about "hard luck when a bloke hasn't got the price of a drink in his clothes," and slouched off. Ransom breathed a sigh of relief, but not till he was safe aboard the yacht did he feel entirely comfortable.

The Erie Canal begins at Albany, but the boys had been told that they had better enter the big ditch at Troy, about seven miles up the river. No sooner had the *Gazelle* come to a stop inside the canal basin than captain and crew were besieged by people wanting to get the job of towing them to Buffalo.

"Take you through for $110, sir," said one.

"Oh, g'wan," said another. "He's robbing yer. I'll take yer through for $75."

"And I've got $20," Ransom thought to himself.

The lowest offer was $65, and at that they would have to tag on to the end of a fleet of grain boats that could not possibly get through inside of two weeks. Every minute was precious now, for before very long ice would form and navigation would be closed on the lakes.

It was a discouraging outlook, but the boys nevertheless made ready for the long trip across the state. With the aid of a derrick, the yawl's masts were taken out, her rigging dismantled and running gear unrove and neatly coiled. By nightfall the *Gazelle* was completely unrigged, and reminded one, as Frank suggested, of a "man whose head had been shaved."

"If you won't pay the price to be towed through, what are you going to do?" Arthur asked when all were sitting in the cabin.

"Tow her by hand," Kenneth asserted.

"What, 400 miles by hand?"

"Yup."

"I'll be hanged if I want to be a mule all the way to Buffalo," said Arthur in a manner suggestive of antagonism. "I wouldn't mind it for 40 or 50 miles, but 400! Well, I guess *not*."

There was gloom in the little cabin that night, in spite of the brightly burning lamp.

With the morning came a friend who was a friend indeed. An

old canal man had read the story of the cruise in an Albany paper and, admiring the pluck of the boys, had proceeded to look them up.

"I'll tell you what to do," said he when he learned of their predicament. "You buy a horse at this end and sell him at the other."

"Buy a horse! What do you take us for, millionaires?" Arthur voiced the sentiments of the crowd.

"Naw," responded the newly found friend with a twinkle in his eye as he surveyed the far-from-fashionable clothes they wore. "You don't have to be a Vanderbilt; you can buy a horse for $20, perhaps less."

It ended by Ransom going off with the man to search for a good, cheap nag. At the end of an hour or so the skipper returned, leading a horse by a rather dilapidated bridle. The beast walked without a limp and seemed healthy; but by her looks one would think that she had more than the stipulated number of ribs—they were so very much in evidence.

"Good gracious, look at the boneyard Ken is leading!" Frank laughed derisively.

"What is it?" Arthur asked mockingly.

"*It's* our one-horse-power engine. *It*s name is 'Step Lively.' *It* is going to tow us to Buffalo, and *it* cost $12, harness included— dirt cheap, sir."

Frank and Arthur laughed him to scorn, but next morning they hitched up Step Lively and started on their way.

ALONG THE RAGING CANAL

"It's 14 miles from Schenectady to Troy,
And that's a blame long walk, my boy."

Kenneth sang as he walked along behind Step Lively, who, true to her name, set off at a good pace.

Arthur and Frank lay back in the cockpit and shouted remarks to the captain on the tow path.

"You just wait," he yelled back. "I'll bet our one-horse-power engine will be fatter when we get to Buffalo than she is now." Forward on the deck house of the mastless yacht was stowed a generous bale of hay and bags of ground feed, fuel for the one-horse engine.

Twenty-five miles were covered the first day, and at dusk the faithful beast was stalled in a shed close to the big ditch, with a plentiful supply of feed. She was apparently very content with her lot, and the scoffers had to admit that, perhaps after all, the old nag was a good investment.

The canal wound its sinuous way through the beautiful Mohawk Valley, the land of Goshen of the Empire State; great undulating fields of cultivated land lay on either side of the narrow strip of water. Step Lively's slow but steady pace gave the boys a full opportunity to see the country through which they were passing and they agreed that it was well worth coming so far to view.

Each took a turn driving the horse, one hour on and two hours off, watch and watch all day. At night the old mare was comfortably bedded down in some old barn on the canal bank and all hands slept undisturbed.

"Step Lively knew the canal much better than did the boys, for she had been over the towpath many times, and driving meant little more than keeping her at a steady, even pace, which, though slow, ate up the miles at a satisfactory rate.

"Let's see, who runs the engine first today?" Ransom looked around at the other two one morning.

"Not I," said Arthur. "I held the throttle the last hour and put her up for the night."

"Nor I," protested Frank. "I tended sheet and was at the helm the hour before."

"Well, then, I suppose it's up to me to handle the ribbons," and Kenneth stepped ashore to start the old mare on her day's work. "You've got your metaphors well mixed up; a fellow overhearing us talk wouldn't tell whether we had a locomotive, a boat or a horse to tow us."

In spite of the parleying the *Gazelle* was soon moving along once more. Ransom walked behind the mare, reins in hand, or walked just ahead, setting the pace. The long line stretched behind, sagging in the water, making long ripples on the placid water ahead of the yacht's keen prow. Frank, with his hand on the tiller, kept the boat in the middle, while Arthur, having nothing else to do, lay prone, basking in the sun.

"Say, Art," Frank inquired drowsily, "did Ken read to you that part of his father's letter where he warned us not to get wrecked on the canal?"

"Yes, " the other answered, "and I thought it the most foolish piece of advice I ever heard. Wrecked in this old ditch! I would as soon think of being wrecked in a bathtub!"

But later they both had cause to remember the warning.

When the hour was up, Kenneth came aboard, Frank took the reins and Arthur his place at the stick. Frank had not been driving long when he met a four-horse team pulling a train of three heavy canal boats. The driver stopped accommodatingly and allowed his tow line to sag so Step Lively and the yacht could pass over it.

Frank thanked him and went over, but hardly had the mare's heels got over the stranger's line than he whipped up and tightened it. Kenneth, who was watching, said, "Look at this chap, Art; he thinks he is going to snap *His Nibs* off with his line, but you watch."

The small boat was towing behind the larger boat, and the driver of the four-horse team figured that when his tow-rope had passed under the *Gazelle* it would snap up and yank *His Nibs* from her fastenings. Soon the tow-line could be felt rubbing along on the yacht's keel. Then for an instant there was a pause while both teams pulled with all their might in opposite directions. The tow-lines tightened like harp strings and the water was sent flying in all directions by the vibration.

Suddenly the stranger's line parted, cut in two by the *Gazelle's* sharp plate rudder. The four horses almost fell on their heads and the driver, who was riding one of them, barely escaped a ducking in the canal. Relieved of their accustomed burden, the team started off on a run, and the driver, picking himself up, ran after them, swearing loudly, ever and anon turning to shake his fist at the boys. These threatening gestures were received with roars of laughter, which continued long after the runaway team and the angry driver had disappeared around a bend.

All along the canal small stores were kept for the convenience of the canal men and their families. Food was abundant, and therefore cheap, and the boys thrived under the easy life, the nourishing fare, and the open-air exercise. In spite of the eight or ten miles of walking each of them put in every day, they began to get fat. Step Lively also showed signs of her good care; her ribs became less evident, and her coat showed signs of glossiness.

Considerable affection had sprung up in the boys' hearts for their "one-horse-power engine," as they called their steed. She was such a faithful old beast, and did her work so uncomplainingly. It was with real grief and alarm, therefore, that Kenneth saw early one morning that the stall the mare had occupied was empty and the ring bolt to which her halter had been made fast was pulled clear out of the decayed wood.

Delayed by a visit to friends that chance had thrown in their way, the skipper had risen at 3 a.m. in order to make up for lost time. But lo and behold, the steed had fled. Without a horse they could not proceed, and there was not enough money in the crowd to buy another, even at $12.

"We are certainly up against it," Kenneth said to himself as he examined the damp ground for hoof prints. He found a few marks, but these were lost in the lush grass surrounding the stable, and all hope of tracing the nag by that means had to be given up.

A howl of dismay went up from the other two when the skipper told of their loss.

"I bet she's five miles off by this time."

"We'll never see *her* again," was Arthur's comforting prophecy.

It was a very serious situation. Over 200 miles of canal remained to be covered, the cold season was coming on fast, and there was not a minute to be lost if the home stretch of the journey were to be traversed this year. The combined funds could pay for neither tow nor another horse, and Step Lively, their sole dependence, was gone.

"After breakfast, when it gets light," said the skipper, putting his plan into words, "we'll divide up, each will go in a different direction, and perhaps we will round her up."

It was a gloomy breakfast the boys hurried through that morning. The gray light of early morning turned the cabin lamplight a sickly yellow and showed the faces of the boys, frowning and dejected.

While Kenneth was downing the last mouthful of coffee, they heard the hollow thump, thump of a horse's hoofs on the bridge just above them. Ransom rushed on deck to ask the driver of the supposed team if a stray horse had been seen, and, to his utter surprise and delight, found Step Lively on the canal bank, gazing at the yacht as if to say, "Well, boys, I've had a bully time, but let's be going."

The skipper nearly fell overboard in his eagerness to reach the land and see if it was indeed the faithful old beast. Sure enough, there was no mistaking the drooping lower lip and resigned pose.

"Well, old nag, you deserve a ten-acre lot to rest your old bones upon and a lump of sugar fresh every hour, but you've got to get a gait on," and Kenneth Ransom, chief hostler, chief coachman and skipper, harnessed her up.

As the boys proceeded on their journey, the horse developed a bad tendency to interfere, and to prevent a raw sore from forming, a boot was put over the place where the hoof came in contact with the other leg. It became the duty of the boy who drove the last hour, when stabling Step Lively, to take off the boot. If left on all night, the leg would swell and the horse would, in consequence, go lame next day. As a penalty for breaking this rule, it was decreed that the offender must wash dishes every day for a week.

Before the boys had this understanding with each other, the poor old mare started her day's work with a lame leg several times, but after the rule was made their memories improved, and Step Lively was soon well again.

One evening it was Arthur's turn to put the horse up for the night. He did it with considerable grumbling, for he was in a hurry to get below in the snug little cabin. The wind blew around the big deserted barn where the horse was to be stabled for the night; it whistled around the eaves and rattled the loose boards of the walls. At a little distance was an old inn or hotel that was also deserted and stood black and desolate in the gloom. One of the few remaining window panes caught the last gleam of the setting sun and glowed with the redness of an evil eye. Arthur made haste to get aboard, and once below, allowed himself the luxury of a good shiver.

"Phew! That's an uncanny place," he said, as he sat down to the meal Frank had already prepared.

Ransom kicked Chauvet under the table to put him onto the game. "Yes, I hear the house is haunted." The wind howled, as if to confirm the fact, and a puff came down the companionway hatch and made the lamp flicker.

Frank and Kenneth kept up a fire of ghost stories, so that their own hair showed a tendency to rise, while Arthur was visibly unnerved. As the wind gave a particularly weird shriek, Kenneth made a scratching noise on the center-board trunk.

"What's that?" said Arthur, startled.

"What's what?" Frank inquired innocently.

"That noise—hear it?"—Arthur paused to listen—"sounds like a person or dog scratching to get in."

"Oh, it's your imagination, I guess."

"By the way, Art, did you take the boot off Step Lively?"

"Sure!" he answered.

"I'll bet you didn't; too much of a hurry to get out of the wind and aboard."

"I know I did—at least, I think I did."

"Gee, that's a queer noise," Kenneth interrupted the inquiry to say. The wind made a noise like one in torment, and the light flickered again.

"I'll give you two dollars if you go out and make sure. It's up to you, and don't forget the week's dishwashing if we find the boot on in the morning."

The thought of a week of dishwashing braced the mate and, lighting a lantern, he pushed open the companionway door and went out.

Almost immediately he was back again, white and shaking. "Say, boys, saw something queer in there—something white moving around, sure as you're born!"

"Did you find out about the boot?" inquired Ransom inexorably.

"No, didn't wait."

"You had better go and find out."

"I wouldn't be hired to go in there."

"Well, we'll find out." Frank wore a superior air, but he kept close to Kenneth for all that.

The whispers of the wind grew into shrieks as they approached the barn, and as Frank reached out his hand to grasp the door-catch, a damp leaf slapped his face. Opening the door cautiously, they poked in their heads and looked. Startled, they saw a dim gray shape in the middle of the big open space, and as they were about to turn and run, the ghost stamped hard and whinnied gently. Step Lively was glad to see something alive and human.

"Hullo, old beast. Broke loose, did you?" Kenneth was very bold and went up to the horse and felt her leg.

"Boot's off, all right, but we've got the laugh on Art."

"He pretty nearly got the laugh on us," Frank remarked honestly.

"Saw your ghost, old man," Kenneth remarked airily when they entered the cabin. "Tied her up good and strong this time."

"You don't mean to say it was the mare?" Arthur had visions of the guying he was bound to get.

"Yep. Let's call her "Ghost" after this. What do you say, Frank?"

"Oh, quit! I'll wash dishes if you let up."

It was only necessary to say "ghost" to Arthur after this episode to reduce the swelling of his head to the humblest proportions.

Step Lively settled down to good, hard, steady work after her various adventures, and the *Gazelle* made her way over the "raging canal" at a good, round pace.

The boys met many people on the way; some were pleasant and courteous, but a few were inclined to make disagreeable remarks. To these the boys paid no attention, and the remarks fell flat, having nothing to feed upon.

The locks, by means of which the boats passed from one level to another, were encountered at frequent intervals. Occasionally a lock tender would be disinclined to take the trouble to let the yacht pass, and made it as hard for the boys as possible. At one time it seemed certain that both the yacht and a member of the crew would be destroyed.

One afternoon the boys approached the great wooden portals of a lock and blew a horn to notify the keeper that they wished to enter; he was a surly chap and grumblingly set to work to admit the yacht. The *Gazelle* once inside, the heavy wooden barriers were closed, two lines were run from the bitts forward to snubbing posts in order to keep her straight in the lock, and Arthur, with a long, heavy pole in hand, stood ready to fend her off from the rocky sides. Frank looked after the horse, while Kenneth helped the keeper.

Usually the water from the higher level was let in gradually, but this keeper was in an ugly temper and allowed the water to come in with a rush. The *Gazelle*, buoyant, rose light as a cork, and Arthur pushed with all his might on the stout pole to keep her from being dented by the cruel rocks. The water came boiling into the basin, and the yacht rocked and strained at her mooring lines. Suddenly one of them parted, and, the strain being unequal, the *Gazelle* swung sharply to one side. Arthur pushed with might and main, but the sidelong swing of the three-ton boat was too much for him; his pole was caught against the side of the lock and he was jerked overboard into the seething pool.

"Art's overboard!" cried Frank. "He'll be crushed, for sure."

"Shut off the water, for heaven's sake!"

They looked into the narrow basin, but not a sign could they see of him. The water swirled and eddied, formed little whirlpools, dashed miniature breakers against the rocky walls and receded. All the time the yacht swung nearer and nearer the masonry, and the boys knew that, unless he escaped by a miracle, Arthur would be crushed between.

For a minute the two boys gazed helplessly. Then a plan occurred to the skipper, which he proceeded to execute instantly. Taking the broken end of the parted line, all the slack possible having been let out, he stood on the capstone of the lock and measured the distance between it and the unsteady yacht. It was a long leap under the most favorable circumstances, and the handicap of the heavy rope and the heaving deck of the vessel, such a long way out and so far below, made the chances of failure infinitely greater—and failure in this case meant certain death.

For an instant he hesitated, then, fearful lest his resolution should fail him if he waited longer, he sprang over the tossing, swirling water straight for the yacht's deck. With scarcely six inches to spare, he landed with a jar that dazed him for a second. With the line still in his hand, he ran forward and made it fast to the bitts, so that the *Gazelle* once more swung straight in the pool.

"Do you see him?" Frank cried anxiously from the shore.

Kenneth looked into the bubbling water for signs of the mate. It was hardly more than a minute or two since the skipper had cried, "Shut off the water!" but Arthur might have met his doom in even that short time.

"I'm afraid he's a goner," Ransom answered. "I can't see him."

"You can't lose me!"

It was Arthur's familiar voice, coming from below aft somewhere.

"Where are you?"

"Astern here, having a swim."

Kenneth rushed aft and caught sight of the mate's legs thrashing around under the overhang.

With rare presence of mind he had done the one thing that could save him: Finding himself overboard, he swam with swift strokes aft and clung, in spite of the twisting and rocking of the yacht, to the rudder. The overhang protected him from all harm, and beyond a chill produced by the cold water he was unhurt.

The lock-keeper, thoroughly scared by the consequences of his ill temper, tried to make amends by letting in the water so gently that the *Gazelle* reached the upper level with scarcely a tremor.

"These very narrow escapes are trying, to say the least," Frank remarked, as Step Lively once more got going.

"Yes, if we really had any skin on our teeth, it would have been worn off long ago," said Arthur, as he appeared on deck in dry clothes, smiling cheerfully.

While the "one-horse motor" could not be classified as a high-speed engine, the old mare plugged along with a steady gait that covered the miles at a speed sufficient for the purpose. It was a great trip, and the boys agreed that it would be hard to find a better way to see the country.

Many of the important cities of the Empire State were cut in two parts by the canal, and as the boys passed through at the two-mile-an-hour pace, they had plenty of time to go ashore and see things—the great electric works of the General Electric Co. at Schenectady, the optical and camera works at Rochester. Troy, Schenectady, Utica, Rome, Syracuse, Rochester and a score of other towns whose names are familiar all over the United States were visited.

They passed many sorts of vessels carrying cargoes of freight over the great water highway of the state: canal boats, laden with lumber and grain, in fleets, single file, drawn by teams of two to six mules, eastward bound, the water within 18 inches of the decks. Forward on many of the boats was a box-like compartment for the steeds when off duty, and it was a common thing to see the head of a mule sticking out above the deck, "viewing the landscape o'er."

Whole families lived aboard these queer vessels; clothes were washed and spread to dry on the little backyard-like piece of deck over the cabin-house. Sometimes boxes of brilliant geraniums were placed to protect the family from the public gaze, and occasionally, under an awning spread over the cabin roof, a woman sat and sewed, rocking a cradle with her foot.

There was a constant procession of boats of many kinds, floating high as a rule when going westward, but laden down within a foot or two of the scupper holes when eastward bound.

One morning the *Gazelle* passed three immense iron grain boats tied up to the stone-lined bank. They were empty and loomed up beside the yacht like small mountains. Later that same day they would have occasion to remember those boats.

They made a good day's run, and night found them tied up to snubbing posts placed for the purpose. Their lanterns displayed, they went to bed, each with a light conscience and heavy eyelids. The open-air exercise and active appetites made the boys sleep as solid as logs. The grain boats they had seen in the morning came along, towed by a steam barge, tooted for the lock to be opened, and two of the boats passed through, but the boys never stirred.

The third boat was left to her own control, and being without sails or steam, she drifted with the wind unhampered. Unladen, her high sides offered a splendid surface to the breeze and she drifted sideways towards the *Gazelle*. Black and remorseless, she swung towards the little yacht nestling close to the rock-lined bank of the canal.

The grain boat's one human passenger sat sleepily on a great cleat aft and dozed. The boys slept on, all unconscious of their impending doom. Slowly, slowly she drifted nearer, until she touched the *Gazelle*'s sides. The ironclad's bulk was great, and driven by the wind against her tall sides, she pushed the yacht steadily until the smaller boat was hard against the shelving rocky bank. Still the pressure continued, and she began to be pushed up out of the water by the tremendous squeeze.

All three boys were stirred into wakefulness by the first upward lift. The first sound that reached their ears was the groaning of the timbers under the tremendous grip of stone and iron.

Instantly the words of the elder Ransom flashed into Kenneth's mind: "Look out and don't get wrecked on the canal," he had written.

Something, the boy knew not what, held his beloved vessel in its grip. Some tremendous power was crushing his vessel as a strong hand grinds an almond shell to fragments. The tongued and grooved cherry woodwork of the cabin creaked, snapped, and, as they looked, was forced out at the joints by the fearful pressure.

With a cry that was half a groan, Kenneth rushed on deck, followed by Arthur and Frank. The great iron sides loomed above them black and implacable.

For an instant he stood dazed, uncomprehending, then he realized the situation—realized that the mighty floating fabric of iron, forced by the wind beyond the power of human hands and human brains to check it, was slowly grinding the doomed yacht to kindlings. He could not bear to think of his vessel a wreck, and, for a moment, covered his eyes with his hand.

IN THE GRIP OF IRON AND STONE

The great vessel squeezed the yacht even tighter, and the boys could feel the deck under their feet bent upward by the pressure. It was intolerable. Kenneth's vessel was actually being destroyed under him and no move of his could prevent it.

Beside himself with despair and rage, he shouted at the blank wall of the grain boat, and in blind fury put his hands against it and pushed—his puny strength against a thousand tons.

"It's a wonder you boys don't go to sleep after a day on the path." The speaker's head showed over the rail of the barge.

The fearful mockery of his words drove poor Kenneth almost crazy, and he shouted at the man words that had no meaning—inarticulate sounds that voiced his agony.

Still the crush continued until the yacht was forced almost out of water and her deck was squeezed into a sharp, convex curve. The poor boat groaned, as if in pain.

The man on the barge looked down on the terrified boys calmly, stupidly, perfectly aware that by no act of his could he avert the catastrophe.

But still the pressure continued. The boys gathered their scattered wits together and, with energy that seemed futile even as they called, shouted for help.

Then came an answering shout, a sound of moving feet on the

grain barge's deck, a sharp, urging call to a team, the snap of a whiplash. The barge began to slide off and the *Gazelle*, released from the powerful grip, settled down. Kenneth and his friends stood poised, ready to spring ashore when the vessel—her seams opened to the flood—should sink.

With a nerve-racking slowness the iron monster moved away until the yacht was wholly released. With a groan that was like a sigh of relief she settled to her normal water line, bobbed up and down a little, as if to adjust herself to her more comfortable position, and floated quietly and safe.

Kenneth could not believe his eyes, but rushed below and, pulling up the square trap in the cabin floor, thrust his hand far into the bilge, expecting to see the water come bubbling out of the well. He was beside himself with joy to find no oozing seams, no leaking crannies—she was dry.

He shouted aloud to his friends on deck the joyful news, and they came tumbling down, incredulous, to feel and see for themselves.

Again the wonderful little craft had stood the test, the most severe in her varied experience. The sturdy timbers, so carefully steamed, bent and joined together, squeezed all out of their rightful shape, sprang back to their designed lines as soon as released from the awful pressure.

When the commander of the fleet came back and offered to make good any damage his boat had caused, the boys were too full of joy and gratitude to exact any damages. Beyond the started joints in the hardwood finish of the cabin, the yacht was unhurt, and they could not conscientiously ask for money even if they wished.

The fleet captain went off, and as the barge slipped off into the night, the voice of the man on deck came back to the boys: "Ye blamed fools, why didn't ye punch a hole in her and go home like gentlemen on the money you'd get?"

Ruin his boat! Kenneth would almost as willingly cut off his right hand. His fingers itched to clutch and shake the man who made such a degrading proposition.

Once more the crew and their faithful boat had escaped destruction as if by a miracle. Once more the hand of Providence had appeared strong in their behalf, and they were grateful—too much affected to speak of it, except in a subdued undertone.

Soon after this Step Lively made her banner run of 31 miles in one day. Arrived at the busy little city of Lockport, the *Gazelle* began the steep ascent of the series of step-like locks to the top of a large hill and the upper level. Five double locks opened one into the other, one series for descent, the other for ascent of the hill. Each lock raised or lowered the vessel in it 15 or 20 feet. It was a splendid piece of engineering that the boys, after their many miles of canal journeying, could fully appreciate.

"Say, this is easy," said Arthur. "Just like going upstairs."

"Yes, only it's no work," suggested Frank.

"It's like some of the sudden trips I have made upstairs when my father had a grip on the seat of my trousers; that was easy, till afterwards," and Kenneth rubbed himself reflectively.

Beyond the "lock step," as Frank facetiously called the series of water lifts, the canal was cut out of the solid rock. The walls of stone rising sharply on either side of the water, the tow-path was a mere ledge cut between the ditch and the embankment. It was a gloomy sort of place, especially since the rain had fallen recently, the rocks were black with dripping water, and the tow-path slippery with mud. The road where Step Lively toiled along was narrow and several feet above the surface of the water. A strong wind was blowing down the gorge-like cut, making it hard for the old mare to pull the yacht.

Frank was driving and urged the beast along with voice and slap of rein. All went well until the horse stumbled over a stone, slipped, and in her struggle to recover her feet, slipped still more and finally, slid over the edge and plunged into the canal with a mighty splash.

Frank stood on the bank and hopped about like a hen whose chicks have proved to be ducks and have just discovered their native element. He still held onto the reins, and when the old horse splashed towards the bank, pulled with all his might. The sides of the canal were as steep as a wall, and the poor beast could not get the slightest foothold. She gazed at Frank with an appealing eye and struggled valiantly to reach dry ground, only to fall back until all but her snorting nose was submerged.

"Don't push, just shove!" cried an unsympathetic looker-on.

"Why don't you put boats on his feet?" suggested another.

Frank was at his wit's end. He tried in every way to extricate the poor horse from her predicament, but since she could not fly, it could not be done.

The *Gazelle*, carried on by the impetus she still retained, came alongside of the struggling amphibious steed, and Frank threw the reins aboard.

"Well, this beats the Dutch!" Kenneth exclaimed, as the three boys looked helplessly down on the poor beast swimming gamely in her unnatural element—a pathetic but ludicrous sight.

"What the deuce shall we do?" Frank did not know whether to laugh or cry, and his face was curiously twisted in consequence.

"Well," said the skipper at last, "I guess the tower will have to be towed 'til we find a shelving bank and the order can be reversed again."

All hands seemed to appreciate the humor of the situation except Step Lively, and she back-pedaled with all her might. Kenneth and Arthur took the place of the tow-horse on the path, and found it hard work to pull the heavy boat through the water and a refractory horse that insisted on swimming backward as hard as she could. As they strained and tugged, puffed and sweated, they lost the funny side, and agreed that it was "blamed serious." At this juncture Step Lively woke up to the situation and swam with, instead of against, her masters, and then all was lovely.

The people observing the strange procession were very much amused, and they did not hesitate to comment.

"Turn-about's fair play, ain't it?" said one.

"About time the boat towed a while, put her on the path," said another.

At length a sloping place was reached, and the old horse scrambled out. It was hard to tell which was more relieved—at any rate, Step Lively took up her regular occupation with alacrity and the boys went back on board with a sigh of relief. For fear the faithful old beast would catch cold, she was kept going, and so escaped harm.

At Tonawanda, on the Niagara River, Kenneth sold the horse

to a man who contracted to tow them to Buffalo and Lake Erie. And so they parted with Step Lively for three dollars. She had entirely lost her hat-rack appearance, and seemed almost as sorry to leave her young friends as they were to dismiss her.

From Tonawanda the canal followed along the Niagara River. The beautiful, broad stream, smooth and placid, looked little like the torrent a little farther below that rushed madly down the steep incline and then made that stupendous leap.

"Is this the Niagara River?" one boy asked another. Its calmness was disappointing.

At Buffalo the *Gazelle* entered her native waters once more—on lake water, but still a thousand miles from home. It had been 12 days from Troy to Buffalo, 352 miles—not a bad record, considering the one-horse motor.

The boys cast anchor within the shelter of Buffalo's breakwater on October 10, 1899, and looked over the strange, green waters of Lake Erie. They immediately went to work, stepped the masts and set up the rigging for the last stage of their long journey. A thousand miles of lakes stretched between them and old St. Joseph, yet the young voyagers felt that they were almost home.

They forgot for a time that the great inland seas were sure to be swept by gales that would increase in force and frequency as the season advanced, until the freezing blast closed up navigation altogether and the waters, now tracked in all directions by vessels of every description, would be deserted—left to the howling winds, the grinding cakes of ice, and the screaming gulls.

It was a serious situation that stared them in the face, had they but realized it. The sharp gales on the lakes were to be dreaded even more than the tempest on the ocean, for land, never very far off, surrounded them, and a lee shore was an imminent peril.

A mere zephyr toyed with the flag at the *Gazelle*'s masthead as she lay at anchor—too soft to waft the yacht a mile an hour—so it was not strange that Kenneth and his crew forgot for a time that the lake, now so calmly sleeping, would soon rise in its anger and lash itself into white foam. The lack of wind gave the crew an opportunity to visit Niagara Falls, and they took time to drink in a full measure of this most magnificent of nature's wonders—a sight they would remember all their days and the crowning spectacle of their trip.

After a three-day stay at Buffalo, the breeze sprang up, the boys raised the anchor and the *Gazelle*, her sails spread to the freshening wind, sped out of harbor and away on the last lap of her race around the eastern half of the United States.

"Hurrah!" the boys shouted and, clasping hands, congratulated each other.

The *Gazelle* acted as if she felt that her native waters bore her once more, and skimmed along as lightly as the gulls that circled in the clear, cool air. Straight across the lake she flew, sped by an ever-increasing wind, until the point off the Welland Canal, on the Canadian side, was reached. With a snap characteristic of her, she came about and started off on another tack, then stopped suddenly with a jar that knocked the boys to their knees. Hard on the rocks!

There was not a minute to spare if the good yacht were to be saved. With a spring, Kenneth let go the mainsail halyards and the slatting sail came down on the run, while Arthur lowered the jib. It was quick work, but these young men had had sufficient training to decide rapidly how to act effectively.

The sails down, the yacht rested more easily but still she pounded, the waves dashing her heavily on the cruel ledges. Kenneth jumped overboard, clothes and all, followed by Frank and Arthur. Putting their shoulders to the yawl's stem, they pushed with might and main. At length the heavy boat moved and, as in New York Harbor, they pushed, walking after, till the yacht floated clear and they had to hold on to keep from sinking. Through the clear water the rocks lurked just under the surface in every direction, and only by the most careful maneuvering could the yacht be sailed to safety.

The sails were hoisted once more, Kenneth took the helm and, after a time, Frank and Arthur went below to put on some dry clothes. The October wind blew keen and sharp; the skipper, crouching in the stern to present as little surface to the wind as possible, thought he would freeze to death—his wet clothes stuck to him, and the cold seemed to go directly to his vitals.

"H-h-h-hurry up!" he shouted to the boys below through his chattering teeth. "I-I-I'll shake the boat to p-p-pieces if you don't g-g-get a m-move on!"

By this time the *Gazelle* was clear of all danger and was coasting over the rollers at splendid speed.

As the day wore on the wind increased in force, and the lake, true to its reputation, was lashed into waves, both high and short. It was the kind of sea that makes a small boat like the yawl pitch and toss most uncomfortably but, in spite of it all, she made good speed. With a clear course ahead, though the weather was threatening, Kenneth kept on for Port Stanley, on the Canadian shore. About 2:30 in the morning the skipper calculated that the light marking the harbor they sought should be visible, but not a sign of it could Arthur, on look-out duty, see. The skipper, in spite of the tossing sea, shinned the mast, and from its elevation caught a glimpse of the gleaming light.

Coming down on deck, he shouted to Frank at the wheel, "We're over-canvassed; we'll have to take the reef down."

The wind made it hard for him to be heard.

"Reef in this sea? You're crazy, you can't do it."

"We've got to do it," the captain answered. "Art, give us a hand on the mainsail."

The mate obeyed, and together they crawled forward. Dark as pitch, they had to work by sense of touch alone. Each knew the position of every line, every rope, as he knew the location of his eyes and mouth, but the choppy sea made it impossible to stand an instant unaided. Arthur gripped the standing rigging with his legs as he lowered the mainsail, and Kenneth clung desperately to the boom as he began to tie the reef points.

The *Gazelle* jumped and thrashed about like a bucking horse, and the darkness enveloped everything. Of a sudden, the boat gave an awful lurch, and Kenneth heard a sudden thump against the yacht's side and all was still. Instantly he missed Arthur— nowhere could he be seen.

The boat shot up into the wind and lay there quivering while Kenneth, dread lying like a weight on his heart, sought his friend.

"What's the trouble?" a voice called from the other side of the boat. "Anybody hurt?"

"For heaven's sake, where are you, Art?"

"Over here. What's the trouble?"

"My, but I'm glad you're okay. Thought you were overboard."

"Oh, I guess it was that wooden fender you heard. It went over in that last jump."

The *Gazelle* went better under her reduced canvas and reeled off the miles like the steady sea-boat she was.

"Well, we did not see much worse sea on the ocean, did we, boys?" Kenneth had a sort of pride in his native waters, and took satisfaction even in its rough moods.

They were certainly formidable. Short, high, and following one another in quick succession, the waves tossed the yacht about as a man is thrown in a blanket.

Daylight soon came to cheer the young mariners, and revealed the Canadian shore but a few miles to starboard. At two o'clock in the afternoon, the *Gazelle* sailed into Port Stanley. Once safely inside, the wind rose shrieking, as if enraged because the yacht had escaped. For three days they lay at anchor, stormbound— three days that would have been much enjoyed if Kenneth had not been so anxious to go on. Food was plenty and the people kind, but the thought of the terrible winter, whose breath, even now, could be occasionally felt, urged them on and took the edge off their enjoyment in the otherwise hospitable place.

To Rondeau Harbor was a 60-mile run, and when the *Gazelle* pushed her bowsprit past the protecting point of Port Stanley, it looked as if there would not be wind enough to carry her the distance by nightfall. But a fair breeze soon sprang up, and they sped along at a good pace. The lake seemed to be on its good behavior—ashamed of the temper it had shown for the past three days, perhaps. It took little at that time of year to rouse Old Erie to a howling rage. At 5:10 in the afternoon the boys saw that the pleasant mood that had lasted all day was giving way to a very ugly temper, and there were six miles more to cover before shelter could be reached.

"Look at those clouds over there," said Frank. "We're going to have a headwind and all sorts of troubles."

"Sure thing!" echoed Arthur.

"Oh, come off! I'll bet you four to one we'll be inside by six o'clock."

Kenneth saw, too, that there was to be a high wind in the wrong direction.

"Done!" cried Frank and Arthur together. "You're a chump, Ken. All those miles with a head wind? I guess not!"

"You just watch your Uncle Dudley." The skipper meant to do his level best to win his reckless wager.

The goal was in plain sight, and Kenneth took his place at the helm, determined to be on a line at least with those piers by six o'clock. The wind was rising steadily and swinging more and more ahead. The yacht, seeming to realize what was expected of her, settled down to her work and slipped off into the eye of the breeze like a witch. Each minute the wind hauled more and more ahead, until the boat, her sheets already closely trimmed, seemed to sail right square into the teeth of it. The gray bulkhead was yet a long way off, and the minutes were slipping by at an alarming rate. Arthur grinned as he called out, "Five-thirty."

It was a race against time with a vengeance. More than the settling of a friendly wager was involved. The clouds to the southwest had an ugly look, and the line of dull gray showed against the bright blue, as straight as if drawn with a ruler.

Nearer and nearer they came to "the haven where they would be," but faster and faster flew the minutes.

"Five-forty-five!" Arthur called, clock in hand.

"Can she do it?" Kenneth asked himself. Only 15 minutes more, and the black edge of the squall so close. Then the wind died down.

"I told you so!" said Frank, exultantly.

Kenneth knew that it was but the calm before the storm. "You just wait," he said. "You haven't got this cinched yet."

"Five-fifty," droned Arthur. "Ten minutes more."

Kenneth said nothing, but kept a sharp weather eye open for squalls.

"Five-fifty-seven!" called the timekeeper.

Off to port the skipper saw the water scuffed up, as if a thousand silvery fishes suddenly sprang up. "Here she comes," Kenneth said to himself, "and she's a hummer!"

All at once the blast struck them. Whoo!

The *Gazelle* laid over before it till her lee freeboard, high as it was, was buried under, and the water lapped alongside the deck house. The boat fairly flew along, great sheets of spray shooting out from her bow, the sails standing stiff as if moulded of metal. *His Nibs*, towed behind, was almost lost in the smother of spray, and her painter stretched out to the larger boat straight and stiff as a steel rod, without a sag in it. My, she was going!

The *Gazelle* was over-canvassed for such a blow, but she could not stop then.

Kenneth sat at the tiller like a jockey on a racing horse, his gaze fixed, his face pale, his muscles tense. Ready to luff and save his boat, if need be, but determined to drive her to the finish if steady canvas and honest manila could stand the strain.

"You can't do it, Ken!" Frank cried.

"But I will," he answered grimly. "Arthur, keep your eye on that clock."

A STORMY NIGHT ON A SINKING PILE-DRIVER

Plunging, then darting like a frightened deer, the *Gazelle* raced for her goal; the long pier of Rondeau Harbor was just off her starboard bow.

Could she make it by six o'clock?

Frank and Arthur thought not; Kenneth would not admit, even to himself, that he was beaten.

Laying way over before the blast, she rushed along. The water churned up by her bows rushed white above her lee rail; the weather rigging, taut with the strain put upon it, vibrated like the bass strings of a harp, the lee rigging sagging in proportion.

Kenneth leaned forward, his face eager, his hand grasping the tiller so hard that the knuckles showed white through his tanned skin. Frank and Arthur lay far out to windward—as far out as they could get.

"Six o'clock!" cried Arthur, looking up from the clock he held in his hand. "And, by Jove, you've won!"

Rounding the lighthouse pier, the yacht slipped in behind the crib and rested in smooth water.

"Well, old man, I take my hat off to you," and Frank suited the action to the word. "That was the finest bit of sailing I ever saw. Ken, you're a dandy."

Kenneth was still breathing quickly with the excitement and exhilaration of his race with time. His satisfaction in the performance of his boat was secondary only to the pleasure he felt in his friends' praise.

Again luck had served them well. For the next three days a storm raged over the lake that made the boys very thankful that they were sheltered in a safe harbor. This tempest was a forerunner of what was to come—a foretaste of what the young mariners were likely to experience. The sudden storms for which the lake region was famous at this time of year had begun, and would continue until navigation was closed altogether by the formation of ice.

A railroad had been doing some construction work near Rondeau Harbor, and had been making use of a few large scows, a steam barge, and a pile-driver from Detroit. With the closing down of the work, several of the working crew had deserted and left the captain of the boats short-handed. That was his reason, therefore, for his request to Ransom for help.

"Lend me one of your men," said he.

"No," answered Kenneth. "But if my shipmates agree, I'll help you out if you give us a tow to Detroit."

"Sure, that's easy," the other responded heartily. All hands agreed and the bargain was closed there and then.

The wind had calmed down when the strange fleet started out next afternoon. It was headed by the steam barge, then came the top-heavy pile-driver, then a scow and, finally, the *Gazelle* herself, reluctantly following along, as if averse to being in such disreputable company.

The three boys drew lots to see who should stay on the scow; the mate was the unlucky one but, in spite of the protests of the other two, Kenneth insisted on filling the post himself. To his surprise, he found that he had been assigned to the pile-driver instead of the scow and, though he realized that it was hardly fair dealing on the part of the captain, it was not a time to go back on his agreement, so he boarded the pile-driver.

"If she leaks," the captain shouted through a megaphone to Kenneth, "you had better get up steam in the boiler and start the siphon going."

The boy nodded to indicate that he understood and made his way aft to the little house, where he found a small boiler, hoisting engine and the necessary siphon.

"Jove!" he said to himself. "I am getting more than I bargained for."

The run to Detroit was about a hundred miles. A hundred miles in an old tub of a pile-driver on Lake Erie in the stormy season! Kenneth's thoughts were not very cheerful, but he set to work to find out all about the strange craft of which he was captain, crew, engineer and fireman.

Though comparatively smooth when the queer procession began, after sundown the wind began to rise, and the sea with it.

Kenneth, from his post, could see the lights swinging on his own boat as she rolled on the waves. The towering structure that carried the weight of the pile-driver made the craft top-heavy and very unwieldy in the sea. It jumped and jarred, swung from side to side, and spanked the rollers with its blunt bow. From time to time Kenneth sounded to see if his craft were leaking, and was comforted to find that all was dry.

The wind increased in force, and the water rose higher each minute with the speed characteristic of the Great Lakes. The sky was overcast, and the darkness shut down on the rolling waters like a black blanket. The steam barge ahead snorted away, heading into the wind, and the old scow of a pile-driver kept its distance behind. Kenneth felt very lonely and longed to be aboard the *Gazelle*, the light from whose cabin he caught fleeting glimpses of, as she swung a little to one side.

For perhaps the twentieth time he sounded the pump and found this time, to his alarm, two inches of water in the shallow hold. He waited a few minutes and tried again—three inches.

"Phew—this won't do," he said, half aloud. "I'll have to start that old siphon going."

By the time the fire was fairly going there were four inches in the hold, and when steam was up and the pump had begun to throw its four-inch stream, the water had gained two inches more.

With an energy born of desperation, Kenneth piled the wood into the furnace and kept the head of steam up. The old pump worked well and, for a time, held the water even. Kenneth stood in the little house watching the steam gauge while the pump sucked, wheezed and sputtered, and the thick stream gushed overboard.

Again he tested the depth of water in the hold and found, to his horror, that it was gaining despite the steady working of the pump. More wood went into the roaring, cavernous furnace, and the needle of the steam gauge pointed higher and higher. The pump worked furiously, but still the water gained.

Kenneth went out to see if he could get help if worse came to worst. The old steam-barge ahead was making heavy weather of it, and every man on board was intent on keeping her going. Just astern the scow spatted the waves doggedly, her flat bows presenting to the boy on the pile-driver a front black, forbidding and hopeless. Far behind, the *Gazelle* bobbed serenely over the choppy waves.

The wind was blowing hard and the waves raised their heads in anger on every side, determined, it seemed to the boy alone on the leaking boat, to have his life. He looked about for a small boat he could resort to in case of dire need. There was none, not even a raft, but he caught sight of a broad new board. With the deftness of long experience, he knotted a rope about it to which he could cling, and hauled it aft close to the cabin door where he could jump for it in case of need.

There was work to do inside. Moreover, it was warm and light, if lonely. Sounding again, Ransom found eight inches of water in the hold. It was gaining slowly, and he knew that it was only a question of time before the scow's buoyancy would be overcome and it must sink. Above the howling of the wind, the crackling and snapping of the fire, the wheeze and deep-breathing sound of the pump, Kenneth could hear the swash and gurgle of the water in the hold—a sickening sound that weighed on his heart like lead. When the boat rose on a wave, the water below rushed pell-mell aft and came with a thud that jarred the whole structure against the stern; then, tilted the other way, it rushed against the bow, until the boy thought that the ends would be knocked out of her.

"Well, I guess my name is Dennis this time," he said aloud. "This old tub won't stay on top long." The sound of his own voice made him more lonely than ever, as there was no response, no answering voice to cheer and comfort him. Many trying experiences and frequent dangers had been encountered, but seldom had he faced peril alone. He longed for the companionship of his friends.

Kenneth sat on an old soapbox and listened to the dreary sound of the water splashing in the hold, and to the wind-devils shrieking outside. He was utterly depressed and hopeless. As he sat with his head in his hands, his elbows on his knees, he thought that he heard the sound of human speech among the voices of the storm. He sat erect and listened with all his might.

"Ahoy, aboard the pile-driver!" The voice died away in the wind, but again it made itself heard above the din. "Ahoy, there, Cap!"

Kenneth rushed out and forward.

A man was standing on the after-part of the barge, megaphone to his mouth, bawling that they were going to get under the lee of Peelee Island and lay up for the night.

With renewed courage, Kenneth went back to his stoking and kept the old pump going until the waterlogged rolling of the crazy craft became less violent and, finally, ceased altogether.

"Thank heaven, we are in some kind of a harbor!" said Ransom to the man who came to relieve him. He was thankful to his heart's core. Coming on deck, he found that they were alongside a long pier. He scrambled ashore and hurried aboard the *Gazelle*, weary, but supremely happy to be alive and on his own craft again.

The skipper could hardly keep awake long enough to tell the boys his adventures, and he had traveled far into the land of Nod before the other two turned in.

When the three arose, the day was far advanced. The leak in the pile-driver had been found and plugged, the wind had died down, and the sea flattened out to the long, slow swell that bore no resemblance to the tempestuous waves of the previous night. Under smiling skies, on smooth water, the voyage to Detroit was a delight. Many stately steamers passed them, bound to and from lake ports.

In the early evening, the electric lights of Detroit appeared, perched on tall, slender poles. In the darkness they looked like clusters of stars hung in the sky.

"Michigan, My Michigan!" The boys sang in their hearts, if their lips did not form the words. Once more they were in their native state, and straight across to the west lay old St. Joe—so near by land, so far by water.

The anchor down, all three boys got into *His Nibs*, eager to set foot on dear old Michigan soil again. The little boat staggered bravely to shore with her precious freight. Kenneth stayed, and went back to the yacht after he had put his foot down good and hard on Michigan land. The other two boys went on for mail and supplies.

Eager to reach home, they stayed but a day and a half at Detroit.

Under her own canvas, the *Gazelle* sailed up the Detroit River to Lake St. Clair, then across that fine sheet of water to the St. Clair River, the connecting link between Lakes Huron and Erie.

Frequent rain squalls had made sailing difficult and disagreeable, but the yacht made good way and, in spite of the uncomfortable weather, the boys were in a very cheerful frame of mind. In Michigan waters, off the Michigan coast, they felt that they were indeed on the homestretch.

As the yacht was almost entering the river, the mate pointed off excitedly towards the flats. "What's that?" he cried. "Look, Ken, quick!"

A very black pillar, like thick smoke, writhed between sea and sky. The surface of the lake rose in a cone to meet it, and the sky narrowed down like a funnel. All the time it was twisting furiously, and the water about it was much agitated. It moved steadily across the lake in a direction that seemed to lead to the *Gazelle*.

"Great king!" exclaimed the skipper. "That's a waterspout, sure. We are done for if it strikes us, just as sure as shooting!"

The comrades watched the watery column anxiously. They were greatly relieved, at length, to see it swerve to one side, sweep across the lake and apparently go to pieces on the far shore.

"Well, we can say, if anyone asks us if we saw a waterspout, 'Yes, we did. Would anyone else like to ask any questions?'" The mate put on an air imitating the cheap lyceum lecturer to the life.

Just before making Port Huron where the St. Clair River enters Lake Huron, the boys encountered the ugly rapids that make the navigation of this strait so difficult. It was a mile long, and a very trying run for a sailing vessel, even under the most favorable of circumstances. A large steamer had sunk in the channel a few weeks before, nearly blocking it. The wind, strong as usual, was blowing dead ahead. It was a beat to windward with scarcely room to come about; one tack was hardly taken before another one had to be made. By the time the end of the obstructing vessel was reached, the crew's hands were worn through to the bone from the frequent and rapid handling of the job sheet.

"Great Scott!" cried the mate from his lookout forward. "We are running down a steamer!"

Sure enough, a great grain boat was coming in the opposite direction and would soon be upon them.

"It's all right," called out Ransom reassuringly. "We're clear of the wreck now."

The words had hardly been spoken before the wind died out, as if by magic, and the sails flapped about limp and helpless. The great boat had blanketed the *Gazelle* as completely as if a wall had been built in front of her. The current was setting back toward the abandoned steel steamship, and the yacht drifted with alarming speed toward the obstruction.

"I'll gybe her," Kenneth said to himself, "and retrace our steps till we get to the open. Then we'll wait till there are no other boats moving." Aloud he shouted, "Look out, boys! I am going to gybe."

Just as he spoke a blast of wind slipped by the grain boat, caught the yacht and slammed the boom over with terrific force. Kenneth expected to see the masts go out of her, but everything held and she raced along the side of the sunken ironclad, luffed up under her stern and lay quivering but safe.

The *Gazelle* sailed up the narrow passage on the starboard side of the wreck, while the steamer passed to port. The yacht ran the rapids successfully and was soon speeding along over Lake Huron with an offshore beam wind. The 60 miles to the government harbor of refuge at Harbor Beach was covered at nightfall.

The next night brought them to the entrance of Saginaw Bay. So far the winds had been favorable and the water smooth, and the boys made daily steps 60 miles long in their journey towards home.

They longed for home with a desire that amounted to an ache. Neither would admit to the other how much he felt, but it was hard sometimes to keep the tears back as something occurred to bring up visions of the little city on the bluff.

Saginaw Bay had a bad reputation. Storms were apt to bluster about its wide mouth, and strong winds were continually blowing across it. Though the low barometer indicated that bad weather was coming, Kenneth decided that he could not wait, and he pushed on across the treacherous bay. At night, and in a place noted for its stormy weather, with bad weather threatening, it may have been foolhardy to attempt the run, but the spirit that lay behind the *Gazelle*'s motto—Keeping everlastingly at it brings success—made the retracing of their steps to a safe harbor a thing dead against the boys' principles.

For once the reputation of the locality seemed to be false; even the glass appeared to be at fault, for the wind scarcely amounted to a summer zephyr, and the waves were long and smooth.

The other boys were yawning, and at 10:30 Kenneth sent them below, promising to call them if need be. The skipper sat with the tiller over his knees, thinking. There was but little to do—a glance at the sails to see if all was drawing well, and an occasional lookout for other craft was all the attention the business at hand required. For almost 12 long months he and his friends had lived aboard the little craft they had learned to think of as a second home, through strange waters, along unfamiliar shores, experiencing all conditions of climate and seeing all sorts of people. Dangers innumerable had been encountered and passed safely, and now Kenneth said to himself: "We are almost home." The trip had been well worthwhile, he thought. He had gleaned information that he believed he could not have secured any other way, and his sketch book was full of plans of all sorts of craft he had inspected.

In almost perfect silence, surrounded by darkness, he sat thinking and dreaming. A vision bright as a picture appeared in his mind's eye, and in it he saw his future career: a builder of swift steamers and sturdy cargo boats, of sailing craft of every rig, and all was good.

He was so wrapped up in his thoughts that for a time he did not notice the ominous silence, the fitful, light puffs of wind that lapsed between the calms, the sticky feeling in the air, the many signs which bespeak a brewing storm. Not till the mainsail flapped in answer to a change in direction of the fitful wind did the skipper realize that trouble was coming. In an instant, the long vistas of his pleasant dreams disappeared, and he became the sailor of a small boat off a dangerous coast, with a storm threatening.

A puff of wind that made the *Gazelle* quiver came out of the north, and Kenneth, one hand on the mainsheet, the other on the tiller, prepared for the tussle.

In a few minutes the squall broke in earnest and the yacht staggered under it like a man bearing a heavy weight. She was carrying too much canvas, so the captain called the boys. The weather was calm and serene when they had gone below, and they were mightily surprised to find the boat pitching and rolling, and the wind tearing at the rigging as if bent on destruction.

Waking from a sound sleep, and coming from a warm, bright cabin into the outer air where the cold wind devils held their revels, was a considerable shock, and both thought that it was a great deal worse than it really was. The work of furling the mainsail was very difficult and did not tend to allay their fears.

"By George, Ken, we can't last long in this!" said the mate after looking into the blackness and listening to the howling wind.

"Yes, I see our finish!" said the other.

"Pshaw! The *Gazelle* has been through worse than this," answered the skipper. "See the pace she's setting? She's going like a cup defender."

But in spite of his reassuring words, Kenneth was troubled. Their course led them through the trough of the seas, and every minute it seemed as if the little vessel would be engulfed by the huge waves. To turn back was impossible; to steer to one side would bring them on a lee shore, and a turn to starboard would carry them out of their course and far upon the open lake. There was nothing to do but to face the situation, to be vigilant and trust to good fortune.

Home, that seemed so near to them a short time ago, now appeared utterly unattainable. The *Gazelle* rolled along, now sinking deep in the watery valley, now rising high on the top of a foam-crested hill. The motion was sickening and continued so long that it seemed as if they had been forever rising and falling in the heaving billows.

Chilled to the bone, wet through from the wind-blown spray and weary from the battle with the elements, it was like a strong hand stretched out to a drowning man when Arthur shouted out, "Light, ho!"

"Where away?" cried Kenneth.

"A little off the port bow. No, it's gone!"

All three boys strained their eyes to catch a glimpse of the will-o'-the-wisp.

"There it is!"

"Where?"

"No, it's gone!"

The wind beat the spray into their faces and snatched at their clothing.

"There it is, sure!" Kenneth spoke exultantly. "It's Tawas Light—at least, it ought to be there."

On a point of land like a crooked finger, as the yacht rose to the top of a wave, the boys saw plainly the steady, clear gleam of the yellow flame.

Like a tired bird, the *Gazelle* crept inside the shelter and anchored; her crew lowered the sails and dropped into their bunks. Utterly exhausted, they fell asleep instantly, forgetting all troubles.

When morning came, there was not a sign of the storm. The sky was blue and clear, a few fleecy clouds floating serenely about in it, the lake below gently undulating and reflecting in a deeper tone the azure of the heavens.

With the sunshine came new confidence, and the boys laughed at their fears of the night before.

"Let's get underway and hurry home, for we're only a little way off now." The mate was in a very jubilant frame of mind.

For several days the yacht sailed along the coast of the Lake Huron side of the great Peninsula of Michigan, close enough to see its beautiful shores, rugged rocks and dark, almost black, evergreens.

At Presque Isle they put in for provisions. They found a beautiful harbor, but no sign of settlement and no place to buy food. The need of provender drove them forth in spite of a storm, which an unusually low barometer indicated was soon due. It was planned to make harbor at Cheboygan, some 65 miles away, but while passing Rogers City the yawl ran into a calm and floated idly.

Great clouds were banked up to the northeast, which spread rapidly till the whole heavens were overcast. The water had the oily, smoky, treacherous look that precedes a storm. Kenneth ordered in the jib and jigger, and tied three reefs in the mainsail.

No sooner had the last knot been tied when, with a deafening howl, the squall struck them. It was a terrible blast. The *Gazelle*, being without headway, careened before it. Farther and farther she went, sinking until her rail was on a level with the water, and it came bubbling through the scuppers; still the pressure continued. She dipped to leeward till her deck was covered and the waves lapped the deck house.

"Look out, boys! Be ready to jump. She's going over, sure!" For the first time Kenneth lost confidence in his boat. No craft, he thought, could withstand such a test. All hands climbed to windward, ready to jump away from entangling rigging.

Farther and farther she listed under the fearful blast; the water was on a line with the cabin roof now and began to ooze through the oval port lights into the cabin.

With muscles tense, ready to spring away, Kenneth still stood at his post, one hand on the tiller, the other clasping the cockpit rail to keep from sliding off into the waves.

With a thrill of hope, he felt the tug of the tiller, the indefinable touch when a boat is in motion. The *Gazelle* was making way at last! But still her decks sloped at the fearful angle and the squall blew undiminished.

The mate stood close to *His Nibs*, lashed on deck, bared knife in hand, ready to cut the ropes that bound her.

Her deck half submerged, her cockpit partly filled and water creeping through the ports into the cabin, the *Gazelle* surged slowly along. The crew clung on the sloping decks, waiting for the last sickening lurch that precedes a capsize.

HOMEWARD BOUND

The boys did not need the captain's cry: "Look out for your-selves, boys! She's going over!" to tell them that they were in fearful peril. It had come to the time when it was every man for himself, and each looked for a chance to escape.

But Ransom clung to the helm and noted, with an awakening of hope, that his boat was increasing her speed. Little by little she gained and inch by inch she straightened up, in spite of the knock-down blows she got from the blast. Faster and faster she slipped along, the energy of the wind driving her ahead, rather than over. The water was on a line with the rail once more, and the self-bailing valves in the cockpit began to empty it.

Arthur put his knife in his pocket and crouched down by the windward rail, while Frank assumed a natural attitude and began to take a more cheerful view of things.

"Thank God!" exclaimed Kenneth fervently. "We're safe once more!"

"That was the closest call we ever had," said the mate.

It was some time before the white squall let up and, when the wind died down, the boys found themselves off the Hammond's Bay life-saving station. Thankful for the respite, they headed in for the refuge provided by the government.

A channel cut through the solid rock leading to a little lagoon, and through this the *Gazelle* was dragged by the good fellows of the station. It was well that the yacht sought this refuge, for a storm that would have sent the staunch little craft to the bottom lasted three days and held sway over the lake.

The enforced stay was not irksome in the least, for there were a great many tales to tell and to hear, and the life-savers were good fellows. But with each day's delay the longing for home grew stronger, though it seemed as if the elements deliberately conspired to hold them back.

After leaving Hammond's Bay, they went on up the Lake Huron coast. Storm after storm broke over them, adverse winds beset them and squalls dogged their wake, but at last they reached the very tip of the peninsula and passed through the Straits of Mackinac.

The feeling of exultation the sea-worn cruisers felt when the keel of their boat once more ploughed the waters of Lake Michigan is beyond all description. Words could not express the joy and satisfaction they felt.

Before a high gale and nasty sea, the *Gazelle* ran into Little Traverse Bay, the first harbor on the western shore of Michigan. Sailing along the coast, it seemed as if they were almost home— that the bluffs of old St. Joe were but a little way off, and that they had but to fire their cannon to get an answering salute from their friends, the life-saving station men.

Putting in at Old Mission, the boys visited Kenneth's friends for several days, while the storm king reigned outside in his royal rage and bluster.

At every stopping place along the line they received letters urging them to hurry, for the winter season was so close at hand, when no man may sail on the lakes. Their people were anxious to have them home. The long, dangerous trip, the frequent lapses in correspondence (enforced, of course, but no less hard for the watchers at home to bear), the stories of storm and disaster at sea, all combined to wear down the patience and courage of the relatives at home. The long stress of violent weather at the end of a fearfully prolonged journey had worn on the nerves of the captain and crew also, and they all had a bad attack of homesickness. The longing for home when it is near at hand but just beyond the reach is the hardest of all to bear.

A short spell of good weather succeeded the days of storm, and the *Gazelle* sailed out of Old Mission for home. The boys' friends lined the shore and waved them Godspeed, and the three young-sters afloat answered with a cheer, their faces bright, their hearts aglow with anticipation. They were going *home*.

The people ashore watched the little vessel, her white sides and sails gleaming in the morning sun as she slipped off like a live thing, dancing over the short wavelets daintily. They watched till she disappeared behind the point.

Word was sent to St. Joseph that the *Gazelle* was on her way again, and the people of the next port of call were on the lookout for her.

All the newspapers of the western coastal towns had printed stories about the three Michigan boys who had circumnavigated the eastern United States in their Michigan boat, and most of the inhabitants of these towns were familiar with the story and took pride in the achievement.

The *Gazelle* had hardly been out of Old Mission six hours when a storm rose that speedily developed into a hurricane. Vessels of every kind sought harbor—steamships, schooners, whalebacks, every sort of craft hurried for shelter—but no word was brought of the little yawl. She was not reported: no one had seen her since she had sailed so jauntily out of Old Mission harbor.

The papers were full of the havoc wrought, of the shipping damages, and lists and estimates of the value of the property destroyed by the tempest were published, but no mention was made of the *Gazelle*. In neither the lists of vessels lost nor vessels saved did her name appear.

Frantic with anxiety, the parents of the crew sent telegrams along the Michigan and Wisconsin coasts on both sides of the lake, asking for news. Then the papers began to take it up, and in large type they printed:

WHERE IS THE *GAZELLE*?

STILL NO NEWS OF MISSING YAWL.

One stormy morning, after the newspapers had been printing headlines like *GAZELLE* UNDOUBTEDLY LOST, the lookout at Manistee life-saving station saw a small vessel, closely reefed, scudding across the angry seas like a gull. The lookout called to his mate, "What do you make her out to be?" The other shielded his eyes from the sharp blasts of the spray.

"Yawl-rigged, 25 or 30 feet, carrying jib and jigger. Looks like she has only three men aboard—never saw her before."

"Yawl-rigged, you say?" The first life-saver stopped to look. "Thirty feet—sure, that's her. Do you know what that is?" He turned excitedly to the other. "Why, that's the *Gazelle*." Been 'round the United States, pretty near. Papers are full of it."

Soon the news was flashed from town to town that the *Gazelle* was safe. The houses of gloom in St. Joseph brightened, and eyes once dimmed with tears now sparkled with joy. Soon the *Gazelle* herself flew into port and dropped anchor safe and sound.

The people of Manistee turned out to do the young sailors honor.

Again, as if by miracle, the staunch boat had triumphed over the elements. With two anchors down and several improvised ones out she had ridden the terrific gale safely.

Kenneth waited only long enough for the wind to die down a little and to get some very badly needed sleep. Next day the little ship started out again, feverishly impatient to get home.

With gales before them, behind them, battling with them from every side, the dogged crew kept on, ever heading southward.

Late one day, each of the three families received a telegram that thrilled them. "At South Haven. All well!" it read. Only 20 miles away now!

It was over a year since the *Gazelle*, her colors flying, her unstained sails showing white, had sailed out of St. Joseph harbor and yet, in spite of their eagerness to get home, in spite of the yearnings of their parents to have them home, they needed to spend a day in fixing up. Kenneth was determined to have his vessel look good when he entered the home port.

But, alas! With only 20 miles of the 7000 to go, it seemed as if they were doomed to wait yet another day. A gale was blowing and the rollers dashed themselves to spume against the bulkheads protecting the harbor.

"You can't do it," the life-savers told the captain. "You'll never get between those breakwaters alive in this wind."

"Yes, we will." Kenneth's mind was made up. A spirit of

reckless daring took possession of him, and he could and would get to St. Joseph that day.

"We'll do it, won't we, boys?" Kenneth turned to the crew that had never failed him.

"Sure!" was the laconic but all-sufficient answer.

"Shake!" said the captain, and they gripped firm hands all around.

"Put in a single reef in the main," the captain ordered, "and hoist away."

The boys looked at him a bit doubtfully but obeyed without a word. The jigger set, the anchor was hauled aboard and the jib halyards made taut. Slowly she began to make headway, her sails filled and, heeling gracefully to the wind, she headed for the narrow way between the breakwaters.

People ashore shouted and cheered, and the boys acknowledged the salute by waving their caps on high.

"Hurrah for the last 20 miles!" Kenneth shouted suddenly, then settled himself for the struggle to come.

It was a dead beat out to the open lake through the 300-foot-wide channel between the long piers. The wind blew so hard that the spray obscured the piers from sight at times, and it seemed impossible that any vessel propelled only by sails could make way against it.

Kenneth planned to clear the south pier with the first long tack. As the yacht sped down towards the opening to the lake, choked as it was with the smothering seas, he realized he had undertaken a very hazardous thing—that failure to clear the breakwater on that tack could mean instant destruction against the bulkhead.

As they came nearer and nearer the rock-ballasted spiles, Kenneth noticed that his boat was not pointing as high up into the wind as usual, and that no matter how hard he jammed the helm over, she would not head right. Instead of making the long angle that would bring her clear of the end, the *Gazelle* was heading, in spite of all her skipper could do, 20 feet in.

The yacht acted queerly but was making tremendous speed. Nearer and nearer she came to the spiles partly obscured by the spray; nearer and nearer until the very slap and hiss of the waves against them was heard.

The *Gazelle* was pointed straight at a group of logs some 20 feet from the end. Kenneth was puzzled and worried, almost frantic, indeed. Never had his boat acted in this way before.

Despairingly he looked across at the rapidly narrowing strip of foam-flecked water when his quick eye caught a glimpse of the jib sheet caught on the bitts.

"The jib sheet is fouled. Quick, clear it! Lively now, boys!"

In an instant it was done. The sail flew out to its rightful position and the *Gazelle*, like a racehorse that has been pulled in too much, bounded forward, straight for the end of the pier. In a smother of foam, amid a swirl of angry waters, the good yacht dashed into the open lake, missing the end of the pier by a bare yard.

Kenneth could not hear the cheer that rose from the hundred throats ashore, but he could feel it and he was grateful.

A little over two hours later, the straining eyes of three boys aboard a little yacht caught sight, through the mist and spray, of a white tower on a high bluff, and the words "There it is!" passed from mouth to mouth. Soon a fringe of people could be made out on top of the bluff, and some yellow-clad figures on the end of the long breakwater, where the life-savers took their stand.

There was moisture in the boys' eyes that could not have come from the spray, and a lump in their throats that would not go down.

Suddenly there was a movement among the figures on the beach, a ripple in the long line bordering the bluff. A flash of white showed here and there. In three places along the line bits of color waved—red, blue and yellow—and the eyes that watched so eagerly for those colors dimmed so that only a blur was left.

The yacht was sailing gallantly, speeding over the whitecaps in a way that rejoiced her builder's heart. The Stars and Stripes, made by loving hands, once bright and lustrous, now dim but glorious, spread out flat by the gale.

Nearer she came to the harbor entrance, nearer to her home port. The faint sound of people cheering came over the seething sea to the homecoming trio. The steadfast colors waved; the steadfast hearts answered each other across the water.

Kenneth headed as if to cross the harbor's mouth. Past the long pier the *Gazelle* flashed, and it seemed as if the boys could hear the people groan. A little beyond, Kenneth put her helm down, and she spun round on her heel, heading straight for the inner basin. With sheets eased, the water boiling at her bow, the waves flowing swiftly alongside, every stitch drawing, every fiber in the rigging straining, the *Gazelle* raced with the flying spray into port.

Her crew, exhilarated, thankful, jubilant, could hear nothing but the cheers of their friends, while the brave bits of color waved a welcome that had been waiting a long year—the best welcome of all.